Paul

The r . to learning
is both long and never
ending --- but it is
the most rewarding
journey you will make

Regards

[signature]

20/11/2008.

The Quantum Leap to Payback Consultative Selling

by

Tony Stocker and
Nigel Lawton

authorHOUSE®

AuthorHouse™ UK Ltd.
500 Avebury Boulevard
Central Milton Keynes, MK9 2BE
www.authorhouse.co.uk
Phone: 08001974150

First published by AuthorHouse 6/11/2008

ISBN: 978-1-4343-8073-9 (sc)

Library of Congress Control Number: 2008903647

Printed in the United States of America
Bloomington, Indiana

This book is printed on acid-free paper.

COMMENDATIONS

"This business book is ahead of its time. As a Managing Director of some 30 years within the competitive arena of Materials Handling, I wholeheartedly both recommend and applaud the principles of this publication. Adapting Payback Consultative Selling is a quantum leap from all traditional approaches and, when fully embraced, delivers high value to customers, all human resources and shareholders alike. Its principles require changes to many processes, including management, sales, marketing and support, particularly in the way in which they think and act, changes which have to come if the role of selling through people is to continue profitably. Well done ESP!"

Larry Blackwell, former MD of Atlet UK

"JDSU's EMEA sales force has worked closely with ESP to integrate their innovative Payback Consultative Selling methodology into our sales process. I wholeheartedly recommend this approach for any company looking to upgrade their selling activities with a more collaborative customer engagement model," said **Sinclair Vass, Sales Director, Optical Comms EMEA at JDS Uniphase GmBh**. "ESP's approach helps companies and their key clients identify and solve business problems that can in turn provide measurable financial benefits to both parties."

"Our sales force is by far the biggest overhead line in our P&L. In an environment of increased globalisation, automation and competition our people have had to learn new skills and techniques to enable our company to outperform the market

1

and, frankly, to justify our continued investment in a large, global, sales force. We can use technology to issue quotations so we have schooled our sales force in ESP's methodology to identify and create value: they and DLL have prospered as a result."

Neal Garnett, CFO, De Lage Landen Leasing, GBU Materials Handling & Construction

"Our business is all about effecting significant change into large sales organisations with maximum impact. By using ESP's Payback Consultative Selling we enable our customers' sales teams to clearly differentiate themselves against the competition. For example, in 2007 over 200 field sales professionals at DHL Express were re-trained in Advanced ROI selling techniques using bespoke Payback Consultative Selling. Value Selling is the standard in today's market, ESP take it to the next level!"

Nigel Bolt, Managing Director, NJB International

"The advice we have received from ESP has been invaluable in training our sales staff and creating win-win relationships with our clients. By truly understanding the intricacies of Payback Consultative Selling and the processes that support the ESPIRE model, we have benefited immensely. Of course, this is a continuous process of learning, however, by continuing to work with ESP we hope to achieve all of our objectives."

Tony de Vizio, Sales and Marketing Director, Dynamis Plc

"During the September 2007 Global Sales Meeting where we recognise the top performing sales employees, I'm struck by two thoughts; I see the same core group of individuals getting up each year and the percentage of top performers is growing. I realise this is no accident and the performance differentiators are clear; the sales employees who have a documented plan, apply a disciplined consultative selling approach and rigorously execute on their goals are the top performers. They out manoeuvre the competition; are in control of the sales process and ultimately year after year exceed their quota. These sales people work in partnership with our customers to achieve a win-win outcome. The key performance differentiators are based upon ESP's overall philosophy of Payback Consultative Selling."

Peter Collingwood, VP CommTest, JDSU EMEA

"The key to success as a sales person/organisation is to truly understand what the customer's needs are and positioning your brand to deliver on these. If a sales person can see themselves as being in the problem solving business, the results can be outstanding. Payback Consultative Selling gives you a clear structured process to follow to enable you to really connect with your customers and drive mutually beneficial outcomes!"

**Tony Iacono,
Integrated Healthcare Business Manager, Astra Zeneca**

"The forklift industry is highly competitive and differentiation is key to maintaining volumes and margin. Differentiation can be achieved by adding application and support expertise at the point of sale which can be presented as measurable financial value to the customer. Payback Consultative Selling is the key to achieving this and we have no reservations in recommending its embracement."

Terry Foreman,
Mitsubishi Caterpillar Forklifts Europe

" "I don't particularly like training companies, and I expect all my sales managers to coach their people on selling skills!" These were my first words to the ESP Principals upon introduction. Nonetheless, I now sit here reflecting back on our 5 year partnership and I am a convert. The disciplined application of the ESP Payback Consultative Selling and Negotiating Process by our top performing sales employees delivers predictable double-digit growth whilst at the same time a profitable win-win outcome for JDSU and our Customers."

Emma Robertson, HR Director, JDSU

"We sell high value IT solutions to some of the largest global organisations and ESP's Payback Consultative Selling approach focuses on the right questions to establish the potential value of an offering. ESP has created a unique method of evolving lead questions from benefit analysis which we have subsequently conducted on products, services, the company and our people as recommended in their book. This is a must read for any aspiring top earner in the selling profession!"

Mike Battersby, Associate Director,
TuringSMI Asia Pacific

"Without exception, our sales staff has incorporated the key learnings of ESP's Payback Consultative Selling methodology and as a consequence we have experienced demonstrable increases in both new business and lease penetration. This improvement in performance has been driven by a better understanding of customer needs and selling value add solutions - indeed both we as a management team and our customers see our sales teams as consultants adding real value to relationships rather than 'traditional' salesmen, now delivering win-win solutions to the marketplace. The success of our training with ESP has resulted in Payback Consultative Selling becoming the cornerstone of the strategy of the Division, and as a consequence the initiative is being embraced company wide."

**David Witherspoon, European Commercial Director,
Materials Handling & Construction Division,
De Lage Landen International B.V.**

"What a refreshing change! After 18 years of working in the same market sector I have been able to approach my customers with a renewed enthusiasm and confidence. The whole sales team found the ESP Payback Consultative Selling programme interesting, bespoke and relevant to our ever changing industrial climate in the UK. Our 2008 budget shows a 17% growth forecast as a result of successfully applying the principles of Payback Consultative Selling in 2007."

Carle Norton, Sales Manager, Koyo (UK) Ltd.

"Working with ESP has increased our sales, secured long term customers and motivated our staff. They are committed to delivering full value add training and totally engage on improving your business model. Highly recommended."

Paul McCloskey, Sales Director, Microlease

"Payback Consultative Selling methodology has enabled the sales force to move from selling the benefits of the product to the Engineering Department to NOW INCLUDE delivering measurable value to the financial community ... a quantum leap."

David Knights, Worldwide Channel Manager, Agilent Technologies

CONTENTS

COMMENDATIONS 1

WHO WOULD BENEFIT FROM THIS BOOK AND WHY? .. 11

    Sales Professionals 11

    Sales Management 12

FOREWORD 13

ACKNOWLEDGMENTS 17

PREFACE 18

    ESP - The Company and Its People 20

INTRODUCTION.. 29

PART ONE - PRE FACE TO FACE PREPARATION

    EXERCISES 42

    Benefit Analysis 43

    Lead Question Generation 58

    Strong Benefit Statement 71

PART TWO - THE CONNECTION BETWEEN BENEFITS,

    VALUE AND PAYBACK.. 83

    Key Notes from Part Two....................................... 89

PART THREE - THE RECIPE FOR A SALE 91

    Key Notes from Part Three...................................... 98

PART FOUR - ESP PAYBACK CONSULTATIVE SELLING

    PROCESS - ESPIRE® 100

    Key Notes from Part Four 104

    Review of Parts One to Four.................................. 106

PART FIVE - E - ESTABLISHING RAPPORT AND

    INDENTIFYING SPONSORS................................. 108

    E   ESTABLISH RAPPORT – Identify Sponsors 112

PART SIX - S - SITUATION ANALYSIS – ANALYSING

    CUSTOMERS' OPERATING CIRCUMSTANCES 114

PART SEVEN - P - PROBLEMS AND THEIR IMPACT....... 118

  P   PROBLEMS – Current Methods 118

  I   IMPACT OF PROBLEMS - People, Customers,

      P&L 121

  Review of Parts Five to Seven 125

PART EIGHT - R - RESOLUTION OPTIONS........................ 127

  R   RESOLUTION OPTIONS – Application &

      Results 129

  Review of Part Eight 133

Part NINE - Economic PAYBACK PROPOSALS 135

  E   ECONOMIC PAYBACK - Financial Benefits

      to P&L 136

  The Executive Summary 140

  Summary of Customer Situation / Needs 141

  Description of Product/Service Application 142

  Business Case 142

  Details of Non-Economic Benefits 147

  Pricing or Leasing/Rental Rates 148

  Contract/Terms and Conditions 148

  Review of Part Nine 149

PART TEN - DEMONSTRATING PAYBACK TO CLOSE

  SALES 150

  Benefit Analysis of Golf Membership 159

  Golf Guest Situation Analysis 169

  Economic Payback Proposal - Golf Professional

      (orally) 170

  Review of Part Ten 173

PART ELEVEN - SUCCESS PSYCHOLOGY AND ITS

  APPLICATION IN SALES 175

  Attitude 194

Goal Setting 196

Habits and Beliefs 198

The Natural Law of Cause and Effect 198

Failure 199

Time Management 200

Review of Part Eleven 203

APPENDICES 207

GLOSSARY 208

RECOMMENDED READING 213

OVERVIEW OF 'PROFITABLE COMMERCIAL
NEGOTIATING' TRAINING MODULE 215

The World of Negotiating 215

The Principal Purpose and Objectives of the Training
Module 218

PERSONAL COMPETENCY ASSESSMENT 219

WHO WOULD BENEFIT FROM THIS BOOK AND WHY?

Sales Professionals

- The Benefit and Value Analysis model within this book enables the identification of new prospective customers who would benefit from the values of your offering and, equally importantly, those that would not. Saves time and improves business growth.

- Payback Proposals create desire in the Buyer to go ahead due to the investment opportunity for increasing profits.

- Provides Sellers with a process to demonstrate benefits and values prior to declaring a price or cost.

- Provides Sellers with a methodology for improving conversion rates and reducing sales cycles using Payback Proposals rather than Quotes.

- Provides Sellers with the means to improve earnings through increased volumes and margins.

- Provides an insight into the importance of positive attitude and goal setting plus an understanding of the Natural Laws of Cause and Effect, Expectation and Attraction.

Sales Management

- The ESPIRE® model provides a trackable process for time and activity measurement, i.e. trackable causes to create revenue outcomes or effects.

- The existence of Payback Proposals provides information to measure pipeline more effectively and accurately.

- Payback Consultative Selling, even though it may not be necessary to use it in every situation, provides managers with a controllable means of hitting revenue targets, particularly when the going gets tough.

- The knowledge of how success psychology affects outcomes is a prerequisite to creating the right mental selling attitude for all concerned in sales, marketing and management.

Plus many, many other benefits.

FOREWORD

Let me start you on a journey that will take you to a Quantum Leap to Payback Consultative Selling and hence radically increase your professional value with your Customer, your Company and yourself.

Don't start the journey unless you are committed to making some challenging personal transitions through analysing the way you view yourself and your profession; this is not a journey for the fainthearted.

Let me introduce this highly practical book by sharing my own experience of the value of the Payback Consultative Selling methodology.

In the year 2001 the telecoms sector experienced the most traumatic industry downturn it had ever witnessed; this had been preceded by many years of double digit growth which had resulted in a degree of overconfidence throughout the industry and complacency in its sales workforce. I joined a telecoms Test and Measurement Company just before the start of the downturn and assisted many mediocre or underperforming sales employees to leave the Company and, sometimes, their profession.

I guess to some of the readers this sounds harsh, however through making these tough decisions in a timely manner, it ultimately enabled the business to survive and allowed the departing individuals to find alternative opportunities where they could be highly successful rather than have them continue on the path of mediocrity.

During the next 2 years it became evident that the industry was changing the way it made investment decisions and our customer base was requiring us to partner them in producing business cases in the format of value based proposals with defined ROI measures. Even relatively small investment decisions were now being made at board level, and an ability to compare and contrast payback on expenditure decisions was a necessity for our customers' survival.

This situation brought about a realisation that selling on technical specification alone would at best match the downward trajectory of the market; survival meant outperforming the market through optimising our customers' business performance by becoming an integral part of their decision making process. This was achieved through implementing Payback Consultative Selling in the sales organisation, which enabled our sales employees to partner customers to achieve business success.

Whilst the change in sales methodology was an important step, the ability of the sales person to successfully apply their new skills was only achieved through challenging their belief systems and enabling them to shift their own personal paradigms of 'how things should be done'. This was achieved by underpinning the introduction of new sales skills with an understanding of the Psychology of Success as outlined in Part Eleven of this publication.

We now have a sales organisation that is nurtured, valued and respected by the Company and sought by the competition. Payback Consultative Selling enables our sales employees to outperform the competition, build executive level relationships and achieve win-win solutions; we invest time to understand our customer's business situation to ensure we leverage the optimum solution, demonstrating, where possible, measurable financial improvements to their profit and loss account.

My own personal learning which resulted from implementing Payback Consultative Selling into the sales organisation and deeply embracing the principles of Success Psychology provided me with the following insights;

- Learning a new competency is difficult, and only through demonstrating courage, a little humility, and being prepared to take yourself outside your comfort zone will you succeed.

- Your ability to accept and learn from failure is an integral part of success.

- The concept of value is unique to each selling experience and the route to identifying value comes from understanding your customer's circumstances, plus the financial deliverable of your offering.

- Developing sales employees is a challenge. Their egos sometimes get in the way. Don't let this happen to you.

- Change or die. Not every sales employee will make the transition from selling on technical specification (Demonstration Selling) to Payback Consultative Selling.

- Selling is as much about knowing where there is **not** a sales opportunity as well as knowing where there **is** one. Not every situation will result in a sale, and this is part of effective Payback Consultative Selling.

- Everyone becomes what they think about, and learning to focus on what we want rather than what we do not want is a key to success.

This book dedicates the last section to the psychological paradigms, attitudes, habits and goal setting plus many other key ways in which thinking effects outcomes. This section alone makes the book worthy of study and explains how selling and providing value to customers represents ways of giving to receive in a commercial sense.

For the sales professionals who read this book, I encourage you to read it at least twice and practice the sales principles therein, which will enable you to continually professionally develop and accelerate your move into the position of a top sales performer, particularly if you are operating in a highly competitive environment. As a result of this development You win, your Customer wins and your Company wins.

Emma Robertson, JDSU
HR Director (Global Sales), JDSU
January 2008

ACKNOWLEDGMENTS

Many people assisted in various ways with the production of this publication. The authors are very grateful and thankful to the following for their contribution

- The Customers that provided Commendations

- Emma Robertson for the production of the Foreword

- Neil Garnett, Jane White and Ray Lawton for editing

- Sandra Reed for her contribution to the typing and production of the manuscript

- Paul Blackwell and Anne Thornhill for producing the illustrations

PREFACE

Selling as a profession is as old as trading itself. Over the decades, the meaning of selling has changed as have the methods of trading.

The early meaning of selling was associated with vending or the activity concerned with making something available for trading purposes. Showing or displaying wares as a means of creating an awareness of availability represented, and still does, one aspect of selling. The other aspect of selling was concerned with the vendor using words and gestures to both create attention to the wares and to encourage or cajole potential customers to trade or purchase.

Initially, most individual traders were engaged in the process of making a living or, put another way, putting food on the table. The two aspects governing to what extent food was put on the table were the margin generated, and the volume traded. Putting food on the table for a small family is a different proposition than generating sufficient sales volume and margin to sustain the overheads of a substantial organisation and generate a surplus profit on a consistent and controlled basis in a competitive environment. Merely offering products and services at competitive prices which often have to be negotiated is very much a hit and miss affair and, as might be expected, many organisations today 'miss' rather than 'hit'. Put another way, they do not generate consistent profits which satisfy the shareholders or, worse, they go out of business altogether.

As globalisation evolves and technology continues to develop, the business of convincing the right customers to purchase sufficient volumes at the right price to generate a viable return on the operating costs by necessity requires a much more organised and controlled approach to selling than hitherto. Globalisation leads to over supply which leads to slimmer margins which in turn has led to the challenges faced by Sellers today.

Many products and services today are designed specifically for applications in certain circumstances where they will contribute to the customer's business in efficiency terms to improve profitability by either reducing costs or increasing revenue, or both.   The problem is that the customer cannot easily identify the potential business values merely by seeing the products or reading about them in a brochure.

With many sophisticated products and services today, it is not what they **are**; it is what they can **do** in specific situations that deliver the potential values.   Designing, developing, delivering, installing and supporting products and services involves vision, experience, expertise and a whole host of other things and, in many cases, the resources in these areas can also deliver financial 'value', or payback, through their expertise or role to certain customers in certain circumstances if only the customer knew they existed and the contribution they could make.   The way in which Payback Consultative Selling is used to establish how an organisation can improve the profitability of its customers, through the supply of its products and services and/or the application of its human resources, is described in the Introduction.

ESP - The Company and Its People

The Organisation

'ESP' stands for Effective Strategic Psychology, which was established in 1985. Since that time, the organisation has evolved to become the International Training and Management School that it is today. The Company's name, whilst a mouthful, was specifically evolved to describe accurately what it provides. It is worth an explanation, as doing so will provide readers with an overall insight into the deliverable of its programmes and its teachings. The word 'Effective' means 'to bring about in an efficient manner'. 'Strategic' means 'has a philosophy or a nature to operate with plans or aims geared at achieving a specific outcome'. 'Psychology' is 'the science of the human mind and how thoughts and belief systems cause outcomes either accidental or deliberate'. To achieve specific sales goals in today's competitive and global markets, Effective Strategic Psychology is the route map, the tools and the mindset needed to succeed. Most of ESP's customers operate globally and are well known in their fields of operation and it is through them that ESP's approach to selling value has been evolved into the current form. ESP is a Limited Company registered in England and is owned by the Principals. For further details please visit our website www.espholdings.co.uk.

The Principals

ESP has two Principals who between them have considerable experience and know-how in the commercial arena, having held senior posts in sales, marketing and management with corporate companies. This background, combined with their experience developed working with organisations large and small within Europe and the US providing ESP's customised services, makes them specialists in the fields of building revenues and margins in highly competitive environments, using its core unique methodologies perfected over time.

Associates

ESP operates with the Principals and a number of Senior Partners and Associates, who, between them, promote, design and deliver customised programmes for both sales resources and their management. All Associates have considerable sales, marketing and commercial management expertise at senior level, providing customers with experience across a whole range of industries in the UK, Europe and the US.

The Authors

The publications are authored by the founder of ESP, Tony Stocker, and co-authored by its Managing Director, Nigel Lawton, who are the Principals of the Organisation.

About ESP Publications

This publication is the first of two books planned to cover specific aspects of the sales processes, models and methodologies as taught by ESP concerning selling value, known as Payback Consultative Selling. This first publication deals with the selling aspect only. The second aspect of Payback Consultative Selling deals with negotiating prices to maximise margins having submitted a Payback Proposal (value proposition). Information on the contents of this planned second publication is described in the Appendices.

These publications have been written to act as a 'standalone' learning tool for anyone wanting to develop their present selling methods and improve their ability to sell value rather than price. In addition, they provide an excellent refresher tool for delegates who have attended an **ESP** training programme on Payback Consultative Selling.

Acquiring new skills to the point where they replace old ones requires considerable repetition and practice. For this reason a number of key messages, words or acronyms are repeated throughout the publication. Scientists have proven that on average it takes nine exposures to new information to be able to recall it from short term memory.

There are interactive elements built into training programmes to aid cognition that cannot be replicated easily using only the written word. Notwithstanding that, both exercises and projects are included in the publication to aid the learning process, as well as review questions and answers that will facilitate repetition which is the key to learning. Specifically for the benefit of those readers whose native language is not English, we have included in the back of the book a Glossary to explain the meaning of unusual words or phrases. In addition, paragraphs are punctuated with illustrations, most of which depict a consultative seller and his trusted briefcase engaged in various aspects of the **ESP** Payback Consultative Selling Process.

Figure 1 – A Payback Consultative Seller focuses on Value rather than Price

The ESP sales training programmes covering 'selling value' are at three levels: Foundation, Intermediate and Advanced. The latter covers the financial measures of Return on Investment (ROI), namely Net Present Value (NPV), Internal Rate of Return (IRR) and Payback, and whilst these are overviewed, this publication focuses on the principles behind Payback Consultative Selling using the ESP ESPIRE® model. By way of explanation, the main differences in the three levels of programme are the extent to which values are calculated in financial terms and applied to the customer's current financial performance to improve it.

ESP Sales and Negotiation Models

It is important to note that ESP has created and registered two principal models making up the complete process for Payback Consultative Selling. These two models are designed around two acronyms, ESPIRE® and ESCAPE® for ease of recall and application. The whole phrase Payback Consultative Selling® which encapsulates the ESPIRE and ESCAPE models is also registered.

Selling value through demonstrating payback requires considerable knowledge and skill and is the main focus of the ESPIRE® model. The knowledge and skill required is essentially in four areas:

- The potential values that exist and originate from within the Seller's organisation, particularly the people and the company, in addition to products and services

- A thorough understanding about how their target market customers generate margin and profits from an operational point of view and how to obtain this critical information

- How to recognise which benefits will create financial gains to produce value and how to apply them to the customer's operating circumstances to create that financial value

- How to construct and present a value add Payback Proposal to demonstrate how specific benefits will deliver measurable financial values and payback to a customer's existing

circumstances in order to close sales with a
viable margin of profit for the Seller

In summary, Payback Consultative Selling is concerned with
the process of identifying the current operating circumstances
of a customer and how those might be improved from a
financial standpoint by the application of any aspect of the
Seller's company through the supply of its products and
services. Persuading the right people to the extent that they
accept and understand a Payback Proposal to consider how
an investment will improve their profitability is a complex
skill that needs to be learned and perfected to become a true
consultative seller, hence the reason for training programmes
being delivered at three levels.

The ESCAPE® negotiating model is a tool contained within a
separate training programme entitled Commercial Negotiating
for Profit. This programme is designed specifically to help
prevent a sales person giving away margin unnecessarily to
Buyers who have decided to proceed with a purchase at a
certain price but who nevertheless convince the Seller that
lower prices are required to close the business.

Developing the Right Mental Attitude

Readers will first need to decide positively that they want to
develop their skills in the direction of Payback Consultative
Selling in order to motivate themselves to allocate the time,
diligence and patience to re-engineer themselves to the
required level of proficiency.   A positive mental attitude
linked to goal setting and a passion to succeed are keys in
the personal development process.   The last section of this

book is dedicated to explaining how we become what we think about, how our thoughts are the principal causes of outcomes in our lives, and how to apply the principles of Success Psychology.

Clearly, the day of the salesperson who is paid merely to maintain existing customers and follow up enquiries with specifications and discounted prices is passing. Companies cannot generate enough income on an ongoing and controlled basis to sustain this selling method any longer. The salesperson of tomorrow has to be able to create new business in an organised way and on an ongoing basis. The human quoting machine faces extinction.

Today effective sellers need to use the Payback Consultative Selling Process as the face to face value add tactical approach with decision makers in order to outposition and outperform those competitors who insist on conducting their business by providing quotations accompanied by brochures or specification detail. The latter outdated approach in effect asks Buyers to work out for themselves how a product or service might improve their business based on a description with or without a technical specification together with a price. Payback Consultative Selling applies measurable processes for calculating to what extent a service or a product will improve a customer's business in financial terms if, indeed, it can be done via the Seller's offerings.

A further significant benefit of Payback Consultative Selling is that it provides Sellers with a methodology that enables them to generate incremental business outside of that generated from reactive leads. It is for this reason that many companies are adopting Payback Consultative Selling as a means of sustaining controlled growth. Payback Consultative Selling can be applied to almost any industry where the cost of the product or service is relatively high and its application will produce improved results equally in the software and hardware arena as well as capital goods and sophisticated services.

Planning and Time Management

In addition to adopting consultative selling tactics, today's effective sellers add customer and time management strategies within a documented monthly sales plan to ensure focus on new business development as well as existing customer maintenance.

Some sales people inadvertently allow themselves to develop a negative attitude towards increasing sales and margin when the market hardens, competitors get aggressive, and buyers get tough. Sales people tend to build a mental picture which blames products and services, prices and rates, the management, the market and competitors as reasons for justifying their lack of performance. Surprisingly the tools for planning, time management and success psychology are aspects of a sales person's toolbox that are not usually focused on in an organised and consistent way by either the sales people themselves or their management. Part Eleven therefore deals with Success Psychology and its application in sales.

Business Development Planning, including segmentation, identifies tactics and strategies for both new and existing customers based on their potential revenue value. Whilst these important ingredients form part of today's Seller's toolbox, they are not dealt with by ESP as part of Payback Consultative Selling. ESP deals with this aspect in a separate training module entitled 'Psychologies and Strategies for Growth' which teaches people how to have a much greater effect on outcomes by showing them how to think, how to plan and how to implement activities for growth.

INTRODUCTION

"When can we make an investment with your organisation?" Would it not be a dream to hear a Buyer say that rather than "Your prices are too high"?

Most readers will have enough understanding of the mechanics of a business to know that generating income is the basic ongoing focus, but a competitive environment will usually mean that prices have to be keen and saving on costs is paramount to maximising profits. When sales people quote a price for the supply of anything, small wonder that customers and Buyers are not keen to pay a quoted price and so the game of negotiating begins. Buyers know they have choice and use the 'fear' motive to convince untrained sales people that they will lose a sale if they do not 'sharpen their pencils'.

Add to this scenario that most sales people have targets to achieve, activities to complete other than sales tasks which take up valuable selling time, it is therefore not surprising that many sales people find it difficult to please both their employers and their customers, let alone find the motivation and time to regularly find new profitable customers on an ongoing basis.

Time is the constant challenge for sales people. There are 8,760 hours in a year. On a nine to five basis for five days a week, this reduces working hours, net of holidays, to approximately 2000 hours. Buyers are available for around just 1000 hours of this time and, therefore, that is the maximum amount of selling time available for face to face activities.

Positioning plays a key role today for large businesses operating effectively in a competitive environment. Positioning is about price vs. value. It is about marketing, methods of supply and support. Indeed it is a whole mix of things which represent the recipe to generate a viable return on the capital employed in the face of the competition. It is not the intention to deal with positioning in this book, but readers need to know that positioning is an integral part of marketing, as is selling and they should both be deliberate workable strategies.

Payback Consultative Selling is not about adding tricks of the trade to the traditional representative Seller's toolbox. It is in itself a positioning tool, a business model geared to generating a viable level of financial return on the Seller's 'all up' costs from existing and new customers.

Payback Consultative Selling is as different to the traditional representative Seller's role as is driving a car to flying an aeroplane. There is no halfway stop. You either use convincing financial arguments to sell or you do not. To do so requires a whole different approach. That is why this book title includes the words '**Quantum Leap**'.

Many selling methods have been evolved over the years and therefore in order to differentiate ESP's Payback Consultative Selling methodology we have reproduced a paragraph from a free guide to selling produced by 'businessballs.com' as follows:

> *"Consultative selling involves deeper questioning of the prospect, about organisational and operational issues that can extend beyond the product itself. This*

leads to greater understanding of the prospect's wider needs (particularly those affected by the product), and the questioning process itself also results in a greater trust, rapport, and empathy between sales-person and buyer. The process has been practised instinctively in good sales people and organisations for many years, particularly since the 1970's, especially for concept selling or service solutions selling, driven by competitive pressures, as buyers began to learn as much about the sales process and techniques as the sales people themselves. In the 1970's and 1980's various proprietary frameworks and models were established and many of these remain in use today. The 'Needs Creation' selling approach is an example of Consultative Selling. It is more involving (of the client) than the essentially one way prescriptive Seven Steps method (PSS – Professional Selling Skills pioneered by Xerox in the 1960's) but it is still largely centred on what the supplier wants, rather than helping the buyer."

So what is Payback Consultative Selling and how does it differ from other methods?

The clue to the true meaning is actually in the words. Let us analyse them.

Payback – Means that the customer will receive the cost of the application of the product or service back over time plus a profit in some circumstances. How this occurs and over what time frame is explained to the prospect in the proposal.

Consultant – The Oxford Dictionary defines this as "a person who gives expert or specialist advice in medicine or business".

Payback Consultative Sellers become specialists or experts in applying the benefits of their organisation to a customer's specific business circumstance to enhance that customer's business in measurable financial terms. In order to be able to do this, Payback Consultative Sellers need to know their own organisation inside out in benefit terms and how those benefits might provide value and payback to potential customers.

Payback Consultative Sellers need to have, or develop, knowledge of how companies operate financially from a Profit and Loss point of view. This knowledge, together with the deep insight of their offerings, provides the Payback Consultative Seller with the ability to look at a customer's business to ascertain how any aspect of the Seller's offerings might enhance that customer's financial position by either increasing their sales, generating more margin, or saving on operating costs, or any combination.

After a short while, Payback Consultative Sellers develop an insight into which customers are likely to be able to benefit financially from their offerings and which ones are unlikely to. This improved insight makes an invaluable contribution to 'time management'. Selling to unlikely prospects eats up an inordinate amount of a 'traditional' seller's time which is a major reason for failing to achieve incremental sales targets.

Selling - ESP has over the years defined a meaning for the purposes of its sales training objectives which will provide readers with an early insight into the teachings of this publication. The ESP definition is "convincing prospects to accept the benefits and values of a proposition to the extent that they want to accept the proposition".

Combine the meanings of Payback, Consultant and Selling to provide an insight into what is meant by 'selling value' through Payback Consultative Selling.

The phrase 'Payback Consultative Selling' was originated by ESP. We like it because, without doubt, its effective use generates increased revenues and margins and, in addition, a win-win scenario results. The customer gets payback by way of a return on the investment, the seller gets payback through increased commission, and their shareholders get payback through increased profits – a true win-win for everyone concerned.

Selling involves a series of activities geared to arrive at an end result. Similarly, Process Management involves managing a series of tasks within a process to achieve a desired measurable outcome. Another word for outcome is 'Effect'. The Natural Law of Cause and Effect states that for every Effect there is a root Cause which may or may not be known. This publication focuses on the Causes that will produce a Payback Sale and provide sellers with a control mechanism within which to operate.

At this very moment, there are thousands, probably millions, of quotes sitting around somewhere in the 'awaiting decision' status. A large proportion of these will not lead to orders for the supplier providing the quote. The control lies entirely with the Buyer and not the Seller.

Payback Consultative Selling is concerned with understanding the potential of what benefits products and services can deliver through understanding and recognising which operating circumstances can be improved financially by the application of those products and services. Having established the potential, if it exists, it is then necessary to be able to demonstrate that potential in financial terms to the right people to the extent that they recognise it and embrace the proposal by investing in it. Demonstrating how benefits deliver measurable financial gain is what is meant by Payback Consultative Selling, providing the Seller with a much greater degree of control. When a decision maker sees a purchase as an investment, i.e. they can see when and how they get their money back plus ongoing returns, they do not see it as a cost. Any delay in making the investment is actually a lost opportunity to improve profit. In these circumstances, customers will find the budget or borrow the money to fund the purchase.

Today, salespeople need to know a lot more about how their target market customers trade, how they generate profit, how their costs are made up, and how to recognise where the application of their product and services can or cannot affect the customer's profit and loss account and, if so, to what extent. The business of Payback Consultative Selling is the total understanding of an offering in benefit terms on the one hand and, on the other hand, acquiring and using the specialist knowledge of how to improve a customer's efficiency by utilising the benefits, plus a persuasive ability to convince customers to accept proposals, by demonstrating how profitability can be improved.

People say "No" to a proposition when they cannot see a reason for saying "Yes". So what would be their reason for saying "Yes" or, put another way, making a positive buying decision? Clearly, the reason is simple; when Buyers can see how their lives, jobs or businesses will improve as the result of the purchase, against which the cost is recoverable, they will say "Yes". They buy things because of what those things will **do** for them as distinct from what they **are**. Buyers often decide what they want to buy themselves without much external inducement. An impulse purchase occurs when a Buyer makes an instant decision that something they have become aware of will deliver benefits to them. Shops and supermarkets generate considerable revenues from merely displaying goods to potential impulse buyers. These sales are generated by clever merchandising but with no intervention or costs of a sales person. Once a sales person is added, the selling price has to increase to justify the sales person's total costs.

Benefits have to be used to persuade a decision maker to see a sales person. If they say 'No' to an appointment a potential sale is dead at that point. Figure 2 illustrates a number of points. In this instance the decision maker is a king about to embark upon a battle against a large army. The enemy have long spears, some are mounted, and yet the king is only armed with a sword. The salesman has not been able to communicate any benefits and the king may not know what a machine gun is, far less what it does. Kings of businesses or senior executives are also extremely busy fighting their own battles on a daily basis. These battles are concerned with fighting for sales, increasing margins and cash flow management among many other things, and they are reluctant to refocus their attention away from these critical activities just to see a sales person. Everything we say or do moves us either closer to or further away from a potential sale. Telling customers what something **'is'** in isolation is risky. We must show how our offering improves their circumstances either physically, financially or both.

Figure 2 – Customers will say 'No' unless they can see reasons to say 'Yes'

So, in summary, customers buy sometimes through a process of working out for themselves when something will deliver what they perceive to be benefits to them as the result of the purchase.   Payback Consultative Selling is the process of identifying potential customers and, rather than letting them work out for themselves that they should purchase, demonstrating just how the purchase will deliver financial benefits to the customer and persuading them to do so. In order to be able to do this, Sellers need to understand much more about how potential customers either live or operate a business to be able to identify how and to what extent the application of the Sellers' wares would improve either people's lives or their businesses. If that improvement can be calculated, and demonstrated, in financial terms, then the benefit has a tangible monetary value. In these circumstances, the price can be demonstrated as an investment rather than a cost. With an investment, a return is expected over and above the initial outlay. A cost is seen as a negative unrecoverable outlay of money.

Payback Consultative Selling can be broken down into constituent parts. Learning each part relative to specific products or services and markets provides a process and a methodology for the activity. The constituent parts of the process and how to complete them form the basis of this publication. Each part is covered in a separate section of this book with models and projects to provide learning and practice as follows:

1. Pre 'Face To Face' Preparation Exercises

2. The Connection between Benefits, Value and Payback

3. The Recipe for a Sale

4. The ESP Payback Consultative Selling model – ESPIRE®

5. Establishing Rapport and Identifying Sponsors

6. Situation Analysis - Analysing Customers' Operating Circumstances

7. Problems and their Impact

8. Resolution Options

9. Economic Payback Proposals

10. Demonstrating Payback to Close Sales

11. Success Psychology and its application in Sales

As mentioned in the Preface, ESP has evolved and perfected a complete sales model for use by Consultative Sellers during face to face selling situations. The model is designed around an easy to remember acronym ESPIRE®, each letter standing for the activity that needs to be completed prior to progressing to the next stage, represented by the next letter.

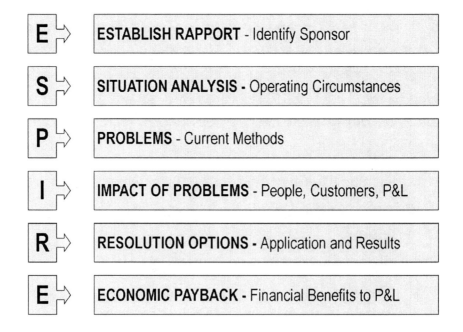

E ⇨ **ESTABLISH RAPPORT** - Identify Sponsor

S ⇨ **SITUATION ANALYSIS** - Operating Circumstances

P ⇨ **PROBLEMS** - Current Methods

I ⇨ **IMPACT OF PROBLEMS** - People, Customers, P&L

R ⇨ **RESOLUTION OPTIONS** - Application and Results

E ⇨ **ECONOMIC PAYBACK** - Financial Benefits to P&L

Figure 3 – ESPIRE® Model

The description of the activity for each letter in the acronym is as brief as possible to facilitate memorising each aspect of the complete model. In order to be able to sell value (Payback) effectively using the ESPIRE® model, it is necessary to understand that Payback Consultative Sellers have to identify the circumstances within which a Payback Sale might be created. These circumstances have two aspects as follows:

1. The Customer having Needs

2. The Seller being able to match those needs with Benefits and Values.

We describe identifying or creating the existence of Needs, plus the ability to match them with Benefits and Values, as the Recipe for a Sale ('Recipe'). The 'Recipe' encapsulates the whole basis of Payback Consultative Selling.

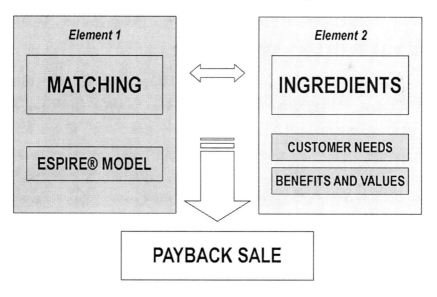

Figure 4 – The Recipe for a Sale

Prior to being able to engage in Payback Consultative Selling using the ESPIRE® model it is fundamental to complete three preparation exercises and these are:

1. Conduct a Benefit Analysis exercise on the Seller's organisation plus products and services.

2. Evolve the Lead Questions for use with customers to establish the potential values of the benefits during the Situation Analysis aspect of the ESPIRE® model.

3. Evolve a 'Strong Benefit Statement' designed specifically to motivate the Buyer or decision maker to willingly answer the questions being asked during Situation Analysis as in 2 above.

We will deal with these three pre face to face selling exercises in Part One but before this, to put the pre preparation work into more context, let us compare Payback Consultative Sellers with Doctors as there are similarities.

Payback Consultative Selling can be likened to the function of General Practitioners (Doctors) in the medical profession. Doctors have to study the human body, learn how illness and disease can reduce the body's capability to perform effectively, and how to treat these negative and sometimes potentially fatal influences. Payback Consultative Sellers have to learn how to look at customers like patients, but only looking for illnesses and disease that they can cure by the application of their offering (Benefits), so to that extent Payback Consultative Sellers specialise and not generalise with cures.

The first stage of learning Payback Consultative Selling starts with cures, i.e. conducting a Benefit Analysis as in exercise (1) above.

Doctors learn how to diagnose a patient to ascertain what is wrong with them. Payback Consultative Sellers have to learn how to conduct Situation Analysis with customers to see to what extent they can improve that customer's financial situation by the application of their offerings.

To conduct Situation Analysis, Sellers need to understand how a customer is currently operating, and they do this by asking specific Lead Questions prepared in exercise (2) above.

One final preparation exercise is necessary to motivate patients or, in our case, customers, to participate willingly with the examination of their current approach to business, which we call Situation Analysis. This preparation exercise is called 'evolving a Strong Benefit Statement' which is used right at the beginning of the ESPIRE® model, i.e. E = Establishing rapport.

PART ONE - PRE FACE TO FACE PREPARATION EXERCISES

The three exercises together with their purpose are as follows:

1. Benefit Analysis
   - To identify the sources of potential value

2. Lead Question Generation
   - To conduct Situation Analysis

3. Strong Benefit Statement Production
   - To motivate the customer to cooperate with Situation Analysis

The three exercises covered in this section only need to be completed once relative to your organisation's offering, although you may modify and sharpen them as you perfect them through use.

Figure 5 – Pre Face to Face Preparation Exercises

Benefit Analysis

The first exercise is called '**Benefit Analysis**' and it is an activity which many seasoned sales people may remember from their basic sales training. Usually this exercise is conducted on services and products only. Benefits are the source of value and therefore the source of Payback and, in this context, the potential benefits to a customer will also arise from areas outside of the product or service. A full Benefit Analysis, therefore, must include three areas for focus as follows:

1. The Products or Services or both

2. The Company, including Suppliers

3. The People, particularly the Sales Person

You will be encouraged later to conduct a Benefit Analysis on your own organisation and offerings, but in the meantime we need to introduce you to the process known as Benefit Analysis and give you an opportunity to complete a Benefit Analysis exercise on a simple everyday item. The item will be a Plastic Disposable Pocket Gas Lighter.

The Benefit Analysis process is conducted by analysing three areas of the item in question.

The three areas are **FEATURES** - **ADVANTAGES** – **BENEFITS**.

The first area of focus is **FEATURES**. Features are facts that can be ascertained by scrutinising the makeup of the item, service or person or by referring to literature and technical specifications. Features are factual and each Feature individually represents one aspect of the whole item.

Before you commence the exercise yourself on a disposable pocket gas lighter, we will first provide another example of how this works by describing how Benefit Analysis would work on an Electric Kettle. This should help you conduct the same exercise on the lighter.

Figure 6 – Electric Kettle

First, we list some of the main Features of an Electric Kettle, so let us review the Features of a typical White 1.8 litre, 2.5 kW Standard 220/240 Volt Mains Electric Kettle as follows:

Features

- 2.5kW Electric Kettle
- 1.8 Litre Capacity
- Automatic shut off switch when water boiled
- Removable 12cm filling lid
- Non-drip spout
- Visual contents indicator on the side
- Colour - White
- Anti scale replaceable heating element

This is probably not an exhaustive list of Features but it suffices for the purpose of this demonstration, however when you are completing this exercise on your organisation's offerings you should be as exhaustive as you can because every Feature may have some potential value for customers in certain circumstances. It is important to note that if weights or sizes are used as Features it is crucial to be precise. For example, descriptions of Features as 'lightweight' or 'small' or 'portable' are words that need relativity and, therefore, will not lead to accurate benefits, unless expressed specifically.

Advantages

Having listed all the Features (facts), the next stage of the process is to work out the ADVANTAGES that each Feature delivers to the user or the customer, which will lead to the BENEFITS. Advantage means the description of the practical deliverable to the user of a Feature.

It is sometimes easier to discover the Advantage of a Feature by imagining the opposite of the deliverable by thinking about what could not be delivered if the item being analysed did not have the Feature in question. For example, if a kettle did not have a non-drip spout then water could be spilled whilst pouring. This could cause damage or injury or at least need cleaning up. Therefore, as the kettle does have a non-drip spout, an Advantage is that it prevents accidental spillage. This leads to the Benefits associated with the avoidance of damage and cleaning time.

Let us now progress the analysis of the electric kettle in our example by establishing the Advantages of the Features previously listed. It should be noted that often one Feature can deliver more than one Advantage.

For the sake of those readers who have not previously been involved with FAB analysis, as it is sometimes known, we will deal with one Feature at a time.

Feature 1   1.8 litre capacity

Advantage   *Enables production of higher volumes of boiled water compared to smaller capacities. A smaller capacity would necessitate more frequent use.*

Feature 2   2.5kW element

Advantage   *Boils in five minutes, which is faster than lower rated elements*

Feature 3   Automatic shut off switch

Advantage   *Negates the need to attend the kettle to switch it off when it boils.*

Feature 4   12cm removable filling lid

Advantage   *Provides the user with a facility to fill the kettle directly from the water source due to its size and the fact that it has a removable lid.*

Feature 5   Non-drip spout

Advantage   *Prevents accidental spillage*

Feature 6   Visual contents indicator

Advantages   *Prevents overfilling*

Facilitates boiling of measurable amounts of water

Shows the user if the kettle needs filling if partial use of contents has previously taken place

Feature 7   Colour - White

Advantage   Facilitates the matching of the appliance with the décor
*[**Note**: In some instances, colour is used for ease of recognition, e.g. red buttons on controls]*

In this example, Feature 6 provided three Advantages, all of which could deliver different benefits to users.

Benefits

As part of the Benefit Analysis, we are trying to establish the principal purpose of the item. In this case, an electric kettle boils 1.8 litres of water fast. Before we proceed to the analysis of Benefits from the Advantages, it would be useful to focus on what is a Benefit and why it is so important for Sellers to be able to identify what they are.

The word **Benefit** means 'what it **does**' for the customer as opposed to 'what it **is**'. What it '**is**', is the **Feature**. People buy things because of what they will '**do**' for them. People have their hair styled because of what it will do for their enhanced appearance, so the styling is the Feature and what the styling does for the person (i.e. improved appearance) is the

Advantage. The deliverable of enhanced appearance will vary from person to person depending upon their circumstances, but whatever those deliverables are, they are the Benefits. In summary, the word Benefit means that it describes the deliverable gain of the Advantage to the User.

As you will understand from later sections, Payback Consultative Selling is opposite to demonstration selling. Demonstration selling is where the customer is exposed to the product either physically or in a brochure. Usually a specification of the product is provided detailing the components, controls and how it works. Prices may also be provided. Demonstration selling exposes the customer to a product or a service and tells the customer all about it together with the cost. The customer is left to think about whether they want to exchange the cost for the product or service, meaning that they have to calculate for themselves what the benefits might be and if those benefits are worth, in their opinion, the price or the cost.

High pressure selling focuses on pressing the customer to complete the thinking process immediately. All sorts of inducements have been evolved to motivate the customer to make a buying decision straight away. High pressure Sellers know only too well that customers left with thinking time will often cool off by focusing on the cost in the absence of perceived or demonstrated benefits. This is the problem concerned with selling Features without Benefits but, more specifically, measurable values. Payback Consultative Selling does not allow customers to work anything out for themselves; that is the responsibility of the Consultative Seller.

Now back to the Benefit Analysis on the electric kettle. Having listed the Features and Advantages, the next stage is to ascertain the Benefits from the Advantages. We have to consider the Advantages in terms of what they deliver to the users, or customers, focusing on what the Advantages deliver, as distinct from just what they are.

You will find that, typically, Benefits deliver similar categories of 'good news' to either end users or organisations because this is what most things are designed to do. Human beings have basic needs or wants, and these are often in the areas of gains, pleasure or protection from loss. In the gain category, products or services are often designed to save time, money, energy, pain, or life. The pleasure category covers a multitude of human cravings, as does the area concerned with protection from loss.

In the business arena, companies and organisations are focused on gaining income, market share, improved image, more gross margin or savings in the areas of cost, effort, energy or risk. The top line activities of profit making organisations are typically focused on these areas and, therefore, the benefits of products and services often impact on some of these. The problem is that users and customers cannot always calculate how products and services impact in deliverable or benefit terms, and it is a mistake to assume that customers can and will do this on their own. Translating what products or services will **do** for different customers in varying situations and showing how these deliverables positively impact on those things which customers are trying to achieve is encapsulated in the business of Payback Consultative Selling. This brings us back to Benefits which are the source of value and, therefore, Payback.

Let us refocus on the Advantages of the kettle and see how they deliver typical Benefits.

Feature 1   1.8 litres capacity

Advantage   *Enables production of higher volumes of boiled water compared to smaller capacities*

Benefits   **Saves time**
                     Saves money

Feature 2   2.5kW element

Advantage   *Boils water in five minutes, which is faster than lower rated elements*

Benefit   **Saves time over slower methods or smaller elements**

Feature 3   Automatic shut off

Advantages   *Negates the need to attend appliance*
                     Peace of mind
                     Negates danger associated with unattended boiling water

Benefits   **Saves time**
                     Saves energy and time from worrying
                     Avoids cost of injury
                     Saves against wasting water as steam evaporates contents

Saves wasting electricity

Feature 4	12cm removable lid
Advantages	*Easy filling* *Facilitates cleaning of the inside of the kettle which extends product life cycle* *Enables access to the element which can be replaced*
Benefits	**Saves time** **Saves money in changing only the electric element** **Saves on the cost of early replacement**
Feature 5	Non-drip spout
Advantage	*Prevents accidental spillage*
Benefits	**Prevents injury** **Prevents potential damage** **Saves energy and time spent cleaning up** **Saves waste of water**
Feature 6	Visual contents indicator
Advantage 1	*Provides 'at a glance' the amount of contents*
Benefits	**Saves energy of heating water that is not needed** **Saves time** **Saves water**

Advantage 2	Facilitates boiling of measurable amount
Benefits	**Saves time**
	Prevents waste of energy and water
	Prevents kettle boiling dry with subsequent risks and costs (safety)
Feature 7	Colour - White
Advantage	Facilitates matching with décor or other appliances
Benefits	**Enhances user's or owner's image due to colour coordinated attention to detail**

The exercise on the electric kettle should provide readers with the process of how Benefit Analysis can be conducted. Try to imagine the extent to which customers might work out for themselves the Advantages and Benefits that they would receive from the Features. You will quickly realise that they would not be able to analyse them fully and therefore it is imperative that Sellers work these out themselves to ensure that prospects understand the deliverables in total.

Benefit Analysis can, and should, be conducted exhaustively, and provides Sellers with the potential value of their offering.

Now it is your turn. The only known way to transfer new knowledge or skills into the long term memory is to practice, as repetition is the mother of skill. When you have attempted and completed the pocket lighter exercise, you will then be ready to complete a detailed analysis of your own offering which, as previously mentioned, includes you and your organisation as well as products and services. At that point, we can move to the real source of the power of Payback Consultative Selling by learning how benefits are translated to measurable value which is the 'Quantum Leap'.

"When benefits are applied to a customer's circumstance, the extent to which they enhance those circumstances is the value."

Here is a picture of some disposable gas pocket lighters, all of which have a transparent fuel tank (Figure 7). This item will be the subject of your first exercise. Approach the exercise from a user point of view, not a reseller or middle man. It may be that you can locate an example of the real thing or, alternatively, buy one as they are cheap enough. Here is what you do.

Figure 7 – Disposable Gas Pocket Lighters

Task 1

Handle or look at the item and, using the table below, list all the Features, or facts, about it. Do not forget to list the items that you might not be able to see, like the spindle on which the flint wheel rotates, and the flint, etc. If you are using the picture of the lighters, use your imagination to assist with calculating how it works and components and Features that might exist. If the item is supplied with an operating manual, review this as well. You would not be able to use your imagination to identify Features on something that you have never seen before, hence the need in these instances to refer to the technical specification and/or user manuals. In the case of software, for example, there are no Features to see on the disc itself and in these instances the specification detail would highlight the Features. In the case of the lighter exercise, you will be able to use your imagination if you are only using our picture because you know what a pocket lighter is and how it works.

Task 2

Think about each Feature and list all the Advantages that come to mind in terms of why the Feature is there, its role, or function.

DISPOSABLE GAS POCKET LIGHTER FEATURES AND ADVANTAGES TABLE		
	FEATURES	ADVANTAGES
1		
2		
3		
4		
5		
6		
7		
8		
9		
10		
11		

At the end of the section, we have listed the main Features and Advantages of a pocket lighter. Compare your list with ours. Can you learn anything from this comparison?

Task 3

Review each Advantage and then list any deliverables that the Advantage provides to the user to ascertain the Benefits. Review what you read earlier in terms of typical Benefits to users, based on human needs or wants.

	DISPOSABLE GAS POCKET LIGHTER BENEFITS TABLE
1	
2	
3	
4	
5	
6	
7	
8	
9	
10	
11	

On the page after our analysis of Features and Advantages, we have listed the Benefits of the lighter. Again; compare your list with ours.

Your next exercise on Benefit Analysis will be focused on your own current offering and we suggest that you complete this exercise later on in this section. Prior to that, it is necessary to understand where Benefit Analysis fits into the overall picture for Payback Consultative Selling. You will recall that there are three pre face to face exercises to complete. Benefit Analysis is the first. Benefits in themselves do not deliver Value. Value is the extent to which Benefits improve the customer's life or their business or both. You will see in later sections when we cover the ESPIRE® Payback Consultative Selling model that during Situation Analysis you are ascertaining to what extent the Benefits of an offering may enhance or improve the customer's life or business and, therefore, provide Payback.

To do this, it is necessary to establish with customers how they are currently operating relative to your offering. Therefore, you need to understand the following:

1. What processes are they using to fulfil a similar function to our offering, i.e. in the case of the kettle, how do they boil water?

2. What are the results of their current process in terms of effectiveness?

3. Would your offering improve the result in terms of saving energy, time, money, etc., and can any improvement be measured?

The second preparation exercise, therefore, addresses the challenge of ascertaining the present way customers do things (Situation Analysis) and requires you to evolve the Lead Questions that would be used to ascertain the potential values of the Benefits relative to the customer's current operations.

Lead Question Generation

In order to complete the Lead Questions for Situation Analysis, it is necessary to review each Benefit and evolve the questions you would ask to ascertain the potential value to a prospective customer.

As an exercise, refer to our Benefit Analysis on the electric kettle and then create a Lead Question against each Benefit using the Table provided. There is no right or wrong way to structure a question as long as you receive the answer you need. You will, no doubt, have heard of 'open' and 'closed' questions. Open questions start with 'Who' – 'What' – 'How' – 'Where' – 'Why'. This questioning technique avoids 'yes' or 'no' answers which are usually the response to closed questions. You need enough detail from the customer's response to be able to judge the potential value of a benefit to the customer and therefore you can use both open and closed questions as long as you obtain the information required. Sometimes, it is necessary to follow the answer to a Lead Question with a supplementary open 'Why?' question in order to establish reasons.

There are no 'rabbits to pull out of hats' or any magic formulas to ascertain a customer's current operating circumstances. You can either improve the way a user or a customer is doing something by the application of your offering or you cannot. What you are doing with Lead Questions during Situation Analysis is to ascertain to your satisfaction what the customer is doing currently relative to the way your offering could do it.

When you have listed the Lead Questions for a potential user of an electric kettle, compare your questions with the ones we have created to check that you comprehend the concept of the exercise.

	LEAD QUESTIONS FROM ELECTRIC KETTLE BENEFIT ANALYSIS
1	
2	
3	
4	
5	
6	
7	
8	
9	
10	
11	
12	

Examples of Lead Questions to Ascertain Potential Values of Electric Kettle Benefits

Question 1   Do you currently boil water?
                  (Based on the principal purpose of the item)

Question 2   If answer to Question 1 is yes, ask 'How do you currently boil water?'

Question 3   How important is it for you to boil water?
                  (Establishing potential value of kettle)

Question 4   How much water do you boil at one time?
                  (Based on Feature 1)

Question 5   What do you use boiling water for?

Question 6   How long does your current method
                    take?
                    (Based on Feature 2)

Question 7   How do you ensure that your water does
                    not boil over?
                    (Based on Feature 3)

Question 8   How do you fill your present receptacle?
                    Does it have a cover or a lid?
                    (Based on Feature 4)

Question 9   Do you spill any boiling water when
                    using it for its purpose?
                    (Based on Feature 5)

Question 10   How do you judge the amount of
                    contents in your present receptacle?
                    (Based on Feature 6)

Question 11   Do you boil varying quantities of water?
                    (Also based on Feature 6)

When you have completed the Lead Questions for the kettle, take your Benefit Analysis on the pocket lighter and list a Lead Question for each Benefit that you would use to establish the potential value to a prospective user.

Again, we have evolved sample questions for each of the Benefits of the lighter which are summarised at the end of this section. Compare your questions with ours to check that you are on the right track.

	LEAD QUESTIONS FROM DISPOSABLE GAS POCKET LIGHTER BENEFIT ANALYSIS
1	
2	
3	
4	
5	
6	
7	
8	
9	
10	
11	

We constantly refer to 'Lead Questions'. You can decide what questions you would ask by pre face to face preparation but you cannot predict what the prospect's answers will be, hence the reference to Lead Questions. Ask the Lead Question and then listen to the customer's reply. It may be that the reply does not provide you with the detail you require, which will necessitate further questions which you construct and ask at the time.

Part Five of this publication deals with establishing rapport with the right people depending on their sphere of influence within the buying process. Different people may gain different Benefits from a particular solution or application. A complete Benefit Analysis should identify Benefits for different aspects of a business and therefore the different people related to those different aspects.

To establish the potential value of one Benefit to different aspects of a business might require a different question related to the same Benefit. For example, a fire extinguisher located in a loading bay of a warehouse may save the life of a store man but it may also reduce the fire insurance premium for the organisation. Two different Benefits for two different aspects of a business from the same application.

Make sure you are comfortable with the pre face to face exercises covered so far before you proceed. Ensure you really understand how to construct Benefit Analysis that identifies clearly what the service or product does rather than what it is. It is quite usual to experience difficulty between identifying Advantages and Benefits. You can conduct Benefit Analysis on anything in your close proximity. If in doubt, take other examples and complete a similar exercise. Try it on a chair, a glass, a pen. It can be done on any man made product. Practice formulating Lead Questions to ascertain the potential values of an item to a prospective user or customer.

When you are satisfied that you have mastered the Benefit Analysis model or FAB analysis, and evolving Lead Questions, it is time for you to focus on your own current offering. Remember this exercise is conducted in three areas as noted at the beginning of this section.

1. The Products or Services or both

2. The Company, including Suppliers

3. The People, particularly the Sales Person (meaning You)

The easiest of these should be the products or services that you are currently selling. In the event that you are not currently selling, choose someone else's product by obtaining leaflets from a showroom or a shop. Commence the exercise of conducting Benefit Analysis on your own chosen offering by completing the following tasks.

TASK 1

List all the Features, or facts, about your products or services. Some products are augmented by services to support the product during use. Some examples of these may be Training, Installation, and Maintenance, etc.

If you are involved in selling services, e.g. Finance, Banking, Logistics, Cleaning or Estate Agency, the task of analysing Features is the same. If your Products or Services have brochures or specification sheets or operating manuals these will often cover Features plus explanations of how they work. These explanations can give a clue to the Advantages.

TASK 2

List the Advantages of the Features using previous examples as a guide on identifying what the Advantages might be. Remember that there could be more than one Advantage for each Feature.

TASK 3

Think about what the Advantages might do for the user in different situations to establish the Benefits. It is quite usual to struggle initially with what is an Advantage and what is a Benefit. Do not worry about this too much as long as the analysis highlights how the Feature translates into what it does for the user or customer through the Advantages or Benefits. Benefit Analysis is the same exercise whatever the industry or product or service.

When you have completed the exercise on your Products and Services, it is time to move to the Company itself. The reason we do this is because often some aspect of the Company might deliver potential Benefits and Values to a customer. The processes used by an organisation to process an order from inception through delivery and invoicing will be of high quality and efficient or not, as the case may be. Some customers value highly different aspects of quality and reliability in the areas of delivery and installation plus any area of pre and post sales support, quite apart from the Product or Service which may be similar to other offerings from competitors.

The more technical or sophisticated the offering, the more focus will be applied to the pre and post sales processes. It is for this reason that these aspects of the Company need to be analysed with a Benefit Analysis exercise.

It is also important to know how the back up services and processes of your organisation compare with that of your competitors. Any uniqueness that you have should be analysed to ascertain the potential values for customers. Does it sound like a lot of work? Yes it is, and it is a lot of work for Doctors, Consultants and Surgeons to learn their trade. The more they know, the more unique their knowledge, the more successful they are, the more money they make.

Benefit Analysis of your company, your offering and the people should be an ongoing exercise. Market Leaders and well-organised business entities that position themselves to sell value rather than price are continually developing their knowledge of the Benefits of their offering relative to that of their competitors.

Having spent time conducting Benefit Analysis on your Company as well as Products and Services, it is time to move on to Benefit Analysis on You. Why do we do this? At training meetings, we often ask the delegates to assess their 'all up' annual costs to include salary, commission, employer's costs (i.e. tax contributions, pensions, etc.), plus expenses including travel and communication tools. It is also reasonable from your employer's standpoint to add costs for an individual proportion of management, administration, office space, etc. Many sales people are surprised at the extent of the resultant figure in terms of overall cost. You might find it interesting to do this calculation in your own case, making assumptions for any calculations where you do not know the exact cost.

Having discussed the cost of a salesperson, we then open up a discussion with delegates regarding their opinions as to who pays for these costs. Clearly, the answer is simple, it is the customer. It is an interesting exercise to imagine how a customer might view this if a quotation were broken down into separate items as follows:

1. A calculation for the cost of a product or supply of a service = £/€/$

2. The proportional cost of the sales person's 'all up' costs = £/€/$

Clearly, quotations and invoices are not calculated this way as customers would surely question the cost of the sales person if they were highlighted separately.

It is nevertheless true that a quotation or an invoice that is pitched from a profit position has to include a proportion of all the company's costs, including the sales person. This is how companies calculate selling prices.

So the question really is, if the customer has to pay for you, what value do you bring to that customer? No doubt you see the point that is being made here!

It is for these reasons that we need to do Benefit Analysis on the sales person, as some of these benefits may bring value and, therefore, Payback to some customers in some situations.

The following story emphasises this point:-

A British cruise ship company had one of their luxury ships completely refurbished at a cost of £30 million. The ship is used for Mediterranean cruises to provide top level luxury to passengers paying £1000 each for a one week cruise. After the refit, the ship was taken out on its re-launch trials with a number of guests.

Unfortunately, the ship had an annoying rattle that reverberated throughout the whole vessel keeping passengers awake at night. The ship was returned to the yard where the engines and the air conditioning systems were stripped out and refitted at a cost of a further £1 million. Again, the ship was subjected to a sea trial which revealed that the rattle was still present.

The world's leading rattle consultant was called in. The specialist walked around the deck for ten minutes and identified a pipe sticking out of a funnel. He took a small hammer, tapped the pipe and the rattle disappeared permanently.

The Chairman of the shipping line was annoyed at the Consultant's invoice for £10,000 given his ten minute attention to the problem and demanded a breakdown of the invoice. The Consultant replied immediately as follows:

Tapping a pipe	£ 1.00
Knowing where to tap	£ 9,999.00
	£10,000.00

The moral of the story is clear. A disabled ship could earn substantial revenues when fully serviceable. The rattle expert may have cost 10,000 but that cost enables the ship to commence earning hundreds of thousands. The difference between the cost of rectification and subsequent revenues is the Payback, all originating from the specialist's skill and knowledge.

You will recall that, in the Introduction, we explained that consultants are experts or specialists. Payback Consultative Sellers are specialists in the area of applying their offerings to a customer's situation to improve that customer's profitability in terms of measurable value. This ability to improve profitability in some instances can be very dramatic. It is the increased profitability that reflects on the value of the sales person in a similar way to that of the rattle expert enabling a £30 million investment to recommence profitable cruises, even though it only took ten minutes. Through his subsequent explanation of his invoice, the rattle expert focused the customer on his real value and not the time, or the cost.

When you learn and adopt Payback Consultative Selling, you have to attain a deep understanding and skill of which 'pipes to tap' using your company's offering to improve the customer's business. You will be able to see from this what the Benefits and potential Values of 'You' would be when you master selling value through Payback Consultative Selling. Once you understand the extent to which 'You' bring Value to customers, you can sell those Values to customers over and above your products or services which differentiate 'You' from your competitors. This focus on value is sometimes referred to as the Value Proposition.

When conducting Benefit Analysis on yourself, give thought to the knowledge and experience you already have in the following areas:

1. Industry knowledge
2. Knowledge of your Company and offerings

3. Your ability to activate your Company for customer benefit

4. Your availability to see customers at their premises to consult free of charge

5. Your expertise as a Payback Consultative Seller to improve the customer's profitability (when you have acquired that knowledge)

Once you have taken time to research all the areas necessary to complete a Benefit Analysis on the three areas of Products and Services, the Company, and You, you are then in a position to move on and list the Lead Questions you would ask prospective customers to ascertain the potential value of those Benefits, i.e. Situation Analysis.

There are a number of mental challenges associated with these pre face to face preparation exercises due to their extensive nature and their complexities. These mental challenges exist because these exercises take most people out of their 'comfort zone'. Out of comfort zone activities require commitment and diligence initially, but eventually they become a new habit and can be easily completed almost automatically. Remember the challenges of using a clutch in a car for the first time. Persevere and you will be very well rewarded. You will learn to work smarter with much more time available. Your value to your employer will rise dramatically because your volumes and margins will move up. You will earn a lot more money with much less effort. These are not idle promises. ESP has trained many hundreds of delegates during the last twenty years, many of whom now fulfil executive roles in large companies, enjoying the resultant benefits.

Having hopefully motivated you to persevere with these Benefit Analysis exercises, we can move on to the last of the three pre face to face projects which provides the stepping stone to the starting point for Payback Consultative Selling and use of the ESPIRE® model, which is mainly used face to face, but equally it can be used effectively on the telephone.

This last pre face to face preparation exercise is concerned with constructing an opening statement to use with prospective customers when you meet in order to motivate them to cooperate willingly with you whilst you establish which Benefits, if any, have any potential Value for the prospect.

Strong Benefit Statement

We call this early stage of the sales process Opening with a Strong Benefit Statement. Some people call it an "elevator speech". Try to imagine your own response if one day you are out shopping and are unexpectedly stopped by a person conducting surveys. What would be your response when asked if you would spare 10 minutes to answer 50 questions? Probably your reply would be "no" in the absence of tangible motivation. Most people would need to understand the benefits and potential values of participating in the survey.

The purpose of the Strong Benefit Statement has already been stated as a means of motivating customers to willingly answer questions. It can also be used very effectively to gain appointments with decision makers.

The source of the content for a Strong Benefit Statement is the Benefit Analysis of your Company and its offering, which you have now completed.

To create a Strong Benefit Statement it is necessary to choose effective words that will be used in your opening which will motivate a customer to cooperate willingly with you when answering your questions.

We have already analysed the word Benefit. A Strong Benefit Statement contains words that explain to customers what the customer will get out of the discussions. What business people are looking for generally is:

- Increased revenue
- Better gross margins
- Lower operating costs
- Increased net profits for distribution as dividends
- Less hassle
- More pleasure and less stress

We need our Benefit Statement therefore to communicate, if possible, how our role seeks to deliver these areas of improvement where we can.

We must remember that we cannot always improve a company's performance, but we can truthfully explain to customers that this is our intent and principal role, and that we are seeking only to establish if this is possible by ascertaining what the customers' current operating circumstances are relative to our offering.

The word Statement means a one way series of words intended to communicate a specific message.

Therefore, a Strong Benefit Statement is a series of words (say 40 to 100) that communicate a message to a decision maker from which they will understand that there are potential real benefits that might help improve their business performance or people's roles.

Review the Benefit Analysis on your Offering, the Company and Yourself, and make your first attempt at constructing a paragraph or two which tells customers what you do and what your organisation does in Benefit terms.

Do not concern yourself with the fact that when you read it out, it sounds scripted, because the fact is, it is! After some practice, you will evolve an opening you are relaxed with that states the truth of your intent, i.e. to ascertain how you might be able to improve a customer's performance and profitability.

You can build into this Statement how your role is geared to improving a customer's business performance.

Example

"Our intent as an organisation is to improve the profit-ability of our customers in measurable P & L terms and to demonstrate Payback on the investment if we can."

Ask existing customers how you being a supplier has affected their profitability. Do they obtain Benefits from any of the pre or post processes in terms of quality or efficiency?

Once you have ascertained this information, which takes a little research, you can build this into your Benefit Statement.

Example

"We improved the sales and margins of Company X as a result of their utilising our product Y in this way. The improvements more than outweighed the costs and they are now pleased to have made the investment."

You need to be careful not to make promises at this early stage of the meeting that you may not be able to keep, so we have to include in our statement our intent to establish whether or not we can do the same for the prospect.

Example

"We are not sure at this point if we can improve your company's performance in the same way as we did for Company X but if you can spend a few minutes helping me establish your current operating methods, I will very soon be able to establish to what extent we can make improvements, or otherwise. May I ask a few key questions?"

Explain how your company is positioned in the market to ascertain if any uniqueness or areas of recognition can be included briefly in your statement.

Be careful not to lead the customer to believe that the Situation Analysis will be a long drawn out boring process which has the intent of setting up the customer for a sales pitch. Customers need to see and understand the benefits of answering your questions from their point of view.

Before we leave the subject of Strong Benefit Statements, it might be beneficial for some readers if we explain exactly where it fits into the opening phases of a face to face meeting. Most sales people like a little preamble after their formal introduction and the exchange of business cards. This preamble is a sensible approach and enables the Seller to avoid an abrupt uncomfortable start to the proceedings. It also provides the Seller with an opportunity to ensure that the person being seen is able to pay attention and that the Seller judges the environment to be satisfactory for a positive discussion. If the Seller feels that the circumstances do not suit the 'ideal', the Seller can make a further appointment.

A typical opening to include the Strong Benefit Statement would take the following format:

1. Cordial greeting with name and business card.

2. A low key preamble aimed at making the prospect feel relaxed. The content should not relate to the purpose of your visit as this needs to be set up properly with a Strong Benefit Statement. Ideally the pre-amble should provide the prospect with an opportunity to participate. The duration of the preamble should be kept as short as possible so as to avoid the prospect feeling that precious time is being wasted.

3. Seller states the reason for the visit by using the Strong Benefit Statement aimed at motivating the prospect to willingly participate in the next stage of the process, which is Situation Analysis.

4. Commence the activity of asking the Lead Questions to establish operating circumstances.

Strong Benefit Statements can be varied according to the position and responsibility of the prospect. Clearly, Financial Directors will have different interests than the Operations Director or a General Manager or Buyer.

Practice different flavours of Benefit Statement with different people with different responsibilities. If you feel relaxed with the Statement, and prospects show willingness to answer your Situation Analysis questions, then the Benefit Statement is fit for purpose. If you do not obtain the required result, you are not convincing the prospect of the Benefits of participating with you during Situation Analysis, so change the Statement until they do.

Part One has covered the three pre face to face preparation exercises that need to be completed. Before we can move to the face to face Payback Consultative Selling Process, we need to understand the connection between Benefits, Value and Payback, and this is the subject of Part Two.

In order for you to be able to revise the three pre face to face preparation exercises easily, they are produced in a short format entitled 'Key Notes'. For Part One, these appear on the next page. The sections dealing with the ESPIRE® model are followed by a Questionnaire with Answers, as opposed to Key Notes.

Key Notes from Part One

There are three pre face to face exercises that need completion:

- Benefit Analysis on Products, Company and People
- Lead Questions Preparation
- Construction of a Strong Benefit Statement

Benefit Analysis

Definition of a Benefit: What the product or service does for the customer and NOT what it is.

The Benefit Analysis model (this is also known as FAB analysis):

1. List all the Features (facts)
2. List the Advantages of the Features
3. Establish the Benefits delivered by the Advantages

Benefit Analysis needs to be conducted in three areas:

1. The Products or Services or both
2. The Company including Suppliers
3. The People, particularly the Sales Person

Lead Questions Preparation

Once a detailed Benefit Analysis has been completed on all areas, we need to establish to what extent, if at all, these Benefits might have Value for a prospect. We establish this by asking prospects Lead Questions.

These questions originate from the Benefit Analysis.

Typical Benefits for businesses are:

- Increased revenues
- Enhanced gross margins
- Lower operating costs
- Increased net profits
- Time saving
- Less hassle
- More pleasure and less stress
- Enhanced image

Strong Benefit Statements

Purpose

To make appointments with decision makers or to motivate a prospect to cooperate willingly and accurately with the Situation Analysis aspect of the ESPIRE® model.

Content

An explanation of the role of the Seller and the Seller's Company to improve the efficiency and profitability of the customer's business (50 to 100 words).

Source

The content of the Strong Benefit Statement originates from the detailed Benefit Analysis conducted on the Seller's Company and the People, together with the Products and Services.

ESP Benefit Analysis - Disposable Gas Pocket Lighter

	FEATURES	ADVANTAGES
1	Flame adjuster	Variable flame size
2	Windshield	External use
3	Flint and striking wheel	One stroke action
4	High impact plastic case	Hardwearing and reliable
5	Weighs 1 gram	Lightweight and portable
6	Size 8 x 2.5 x 1 cm	Pocket size
7	Transparent fuel tank	Measurable use and life
8	3 month guarantee	No risk of downtime
9	Fixed supply of fuel	Disposable
10	Durable components	Reliability for its life
11	3 Colours – Red, Green, Blue	Easily identifiable and matches fashion

	BENEFITS – DISPOSABLE GAS POCKET LIGHTER
1	Flexible application saves money
2	Multi purpose saves money
3	Saves energy and time
4	Saves on breakage and replacement costs
5	Easy to move - saves energy and time
6	Less storage space, easily moved - hence less costs
7	Avoidance of loss of flame and use – insurance
8	Avoidance of failure and replacement cost
9	Saves on storage and disposal costs
10	Saves maintenance and repair costs
11	Enhances image and positioning; ease of identity

	LEAD QUESTIONS FROM DISPOSABLE GAS POCKET LIGHTER BENEFIT ANALYSIS
1	Do you use portable flame in different circumstances?
2	Do you use flame outside in the open?
3	How much time does it take to produce flame?
4	What is the current cost of repair or replacement?
5	How do you currently move your lighting device?
6	What does it cost to store?
7	Have you ever not had the ability to create flame?
8	Have you ever experienced a failure in creating flame?
9	What are the costs associated with disposal?
10	What are your current costs of maintenance and repair?
11	How important is image and positioning?

PART TWO - THE CONNECTION BETWEEN BENEFITS, VALUE AND PAYBACK

The majority of commercial and business people would describe 'Value Add' as a term used when a standard product is added to by way of treatments or extras to differentiate it from similar products and to generate additional margin. For example, let us take the potato. Some retailers will sell it loose by weight. To add value, some retailers will sell them washed and pre-wrapped and charge more. Other retailers will go further and offer them pre-cooked or even stuffed and add more value and charge even more. Many 'me too' products in their naked state are very price sensitive and because they are 'me too', they are then subjected to 'Value Add' for the reasons already mentioned.

The phrases 'Value Add' and 'Consultative Selling' are widely used in the selling methodology field. The definition of 'Payback' within Payback Consultative Selling is specific in order to avoid confusion. Payback Consultative Selling in ESP terms means how the Benefits of an offering may translate themselves into tangible measurable financial gain (Value) when applied to the present operating circumstances of a particular business. The cost will be either partially or fully recovered, as illustrated in the example below. In the event that the cost can be more than recovered, the amount above the price paid represents a 'Return on Investment (ROI)'. In the context of Payback Consultative Selling, Payback equals 'Value Add'.

	Cost		Return			
Example A	(100)	+	50	=	(50)	(Partial Recovery of Cost)
Example B	(100))	+	100	=	0	(Full Recovery of Cost)
Example C	(100)	+	200	=	100	(Return on Investment)

Payback Consultative Selling is concerned with the process of identifying the current operating circumstances of a business and how these might be improved from a financial standpoint by the application of any aspect of the Seller's company through the supply of products and services. Such improvements would be delivered as the direct result of the Benefits of the application which we define as 'Value'. It follows, therefore, that Benefits are the source of potential Value and, as the result of any such Value, provide Payback for customers.

You should have completed an extensive Benefit Analysis on your Products and Services in line with the exercises set out in Part One. However, Value Analysis cannot be pre-conducted in isolation because Benefits may or may not deliver Value dependent upon the circumstances under which the customer is operating, hence the need to link Benefit Analysis with Situation Analysis.

A Payback Sale can only occur when the Benefits of an offering are presented to a customer so that the Benefits show how the offering improves profitability in measurable terms if, indeed, that can be accomplished. Prospects and customers generally have an ongoing need to improve profitability. This Need if matched with Benefits and Value creates the circumstances for which a sale may be accomplished. ESP defines the circumstances for a sale as the 'Recipe' which is dealt with in the next section of the book.

Figure 8 – Recipe for a Sale

In the context of Payback Consultative Selling, Value or Payback means the measurable financial extent to which a customer's Profit & Loss account can be improved by the application of the Seller's offering. The Seller's offering, you will recall, includes potential Benefits, not just from Products and Services, but from any aspect of the Seller's company or its people, hence the necessity to conduct Benefit Analysis on all three aspects of the offering. You will see that the whole purpose of conducting Situation Analysis is to establish how the customer is currently operating in terms of Profit & Loss. During Situation Analysis, you will be finding out how the customer generates sales together with margin on those sales.

This function is carried out under the Problem and Impact aspect of the ESPIRE® model. To establish how the Seller might add Value, and therefore Payback, is a combination of firstly understanding the potential Value of the Benefits of the offering by conducting detailed Benefit Analysis and, secondly, understanding the way these might improve the financial aspects of the customer's business.

Ideally, values should be specified as accurately as possible in monetary terms when proposing that a customer changes the way they currently operate by adopting the Seller's solution. This proposal only takes place during the Economic Payback Proposal stage at the end of the ESPIRE® model. The extent to which the Seller can accurately assess measurable financial gains by accepting a proposal is the extent to which the price of the offering can be presented as an investment rather than a cost. Quite often, it is necessary for Sellers to recommend a change to the way a customer is currently operating in some specific aspects in order to apply an offering to a business to improve efficiency. This approach is clearly different to merely seeking to exchange one product or service for another, although this will also occur in some Payback Proposals.

Finally, it is very important to understand that whilst Benefit Analysis can be conducted in isolation, i.e. in the office, classroom or at home, 'Value Analysis' can only be completed when the full operating circumstances of the customer are completely understood. Training for Payback Consultative Selling is conducted by ESP at three levels, Foundation, Intermediate and Advanced. It is worth mentioning again that the main difference with these programmes is the extent to which Values are calculated and proposed to a customer. We recommend to our customers that delegates proposed for training are assessed in terms of their current experience with Profit & Loss as well as the level in the Buying Process to which they currently sell.

At the back of this publication, a competency analysis template can be found which focuses on four areas:

- Selling and Persuasion
- Negotiating
- Time Management and Planning
- Attitude and Communication

You may like to form a personal view on your current level of competency by completing the 20 question analysis.

If delegates, or readers, are experienced with selling at Board Level by making financially supported business cases, then they should attend the Advanced programme. If, however, they are not familiar at this level, they should attend Foundation or Intermediate training. The sales process we use to train Payback Consultative Selling is similar but each programme deals with more financial detail. Delegates with no previous financial experience should start at the beginning and work upwards over time. Readers should do the same thing. At the end of Foundation training, delegates would be able to show prospective customers which aspects of their present operating circumstances could be financially improved, albeit that they might not be able to demonstrate the precise financial calculation. This approach, however, is much more powerful than merely presenting the customer with a brochure and a price. Learning to sell financially takes time, so tackle the challenge one bit at a time.

The next part of the book deals with the ESPIRE® sales model, which is the face to face methodology we teach to enable sales people to switch from demonstration selling to Payback Consultative Selling.

Key Notes from Part Two

1. The definition of Value for Payback Consultative Selling is 'the extent to which a customer's business is improved financially by the application of the Seller's Products or Services, or both'.

2. Benefit Analysis can be pre-calculated, but Values cannot, due to the fact that actual operating circumstances vary, thereby varying the degree by which Benefits can affect them, if at all.

3. The Recipe for a sale includes the ingredients, i.e. Benefits vs. Circumstances showing Needs, together with a process for preparing the ingredients for the completion of a sale through a Payback Proposal.

4. The role of the Consultative Seller is to establish which operating circumstances (Situation Analysis) can be improved financially by the application of an offering including Services and/or Products. The extent to which those circumstances might be improved is dependent upon the Seller's skill in calculating the application of the offering to the circumstances to improve performance on a measurable basis.

5. Quite often, it is necessary for Consultative Sellers to recommend changes to the way processes are completed using the Seller's offering. This is called 'process re-engineering', and would form part of a Payback Proposal dealt with later in the last 'E' of the ESPIRE® model.

6. Payback Consultative Selling is completely opposite to demonstration selling in the way in which it is conducted. The former requires a whole different set of knowledge about the offering and the way in which the sales call is conducted. Old habits have to be broken so it is necessary to approach Payback Consultative Selling one stage at a time. The first and most critical aspect is to master 'Benefit Analysis' and how Benefits relate to potential Values prior to attempting the ESPIRE® sales model.

PART THREE - THE RECIPE FOR A SALE

This section is dedicated to explaining the circumstances that need to prevail for a sale to take place. However, the existence of the right circumstances in themselves will not necessarily mean that a sale will result. We differentiate the right circumstances for a sale from the persuasion process because they are different and equally important. The right circumstances plus the persuasion process represent a 'Recipe for a Sale'.

In cooking, recipes are used extensively. A recipe usually comprises two elements for a successful outcome. One element of a recipe is the ingredients and their quantities. These have to be exact or the outcome will not be as expected. The other element is the process for dealing with the ingredients, which covers the preparation and cooking. This part of the process is equally important and needs to be completed effectively to ensure a successful outcome.

The recipe for a Payback Sale is the same. The two elements for a Payback Sale have to be correct and the process has to be completed properly. Both of these completely different elements are vital to the outcome. The ingredients for a sale are Customer Needs and the Supplier's Benefits and Values. The Matching of the two ingredients is the process for making a successful sale. The Matching aspect of the Recipe for a Sale is incorporated in the ESPIRE® model which is used in Payback Consultative Selling.

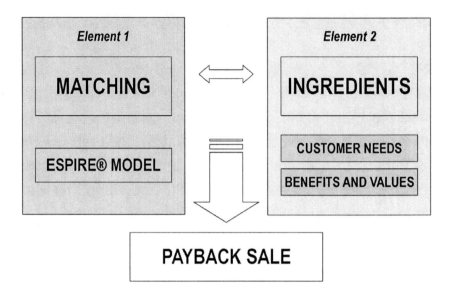

Figure 9 – Recipe for a Sale – Elements and the Ingredients

The role of the Payback Consultative Seller is therefore relatively simple although initially not easy. Payback Consultative Sellers need to identify, firstly, the Customer's Needs as seen by the Seller, and secondly, how they may be matched by Benefits and potential Values. Customers may be experiencing some problems against their objectives but have not necessarily analysed the real extent and cost of such problems. Payback Consultative Sellers analyse the extent of problems and their cost in order to establish the extent of the need to resolve them. Customers like all people have belief systems which are established over time by habit. They are sometimes blind to doing things in a different way. Payback Consultative Sellers learn to recognise, like Doctors, which businesses can be improved by their offering, which is the first stage of establishing the 'Ingredients'. Convincing the customer is a secondary and separate function, which is encapsulated within the 'Matching' aspect of the 'Recipe for a Sale'.

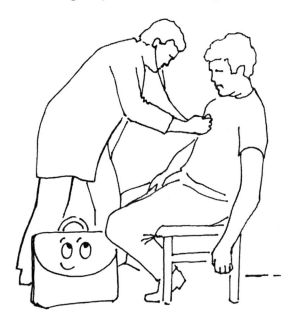

Figure 10 – Consultative Sellers are like Doctors

The ESPIRE® model deals with the entire function of establishing the ingredients (if they exist) and how to convince the customer by making the necessary preparation to convince them by way of a Payback Proposal. Each of the two elements of the Recipe is always approached in exactly the same way using the same process which harnesses the Natural Law of Cause and Effect. This does not mean that sales cannot be created where there is no specifically stated customer need, as they can be created by a Seller using Payback Consultative Selling. What it does guarantee is, if the correct ingredients can be identified or created, and the ESPIRE® sales model is completed effectively, the best possible financial argument for the customer to accept a proposal can be produced. However, circumstances may exist which cannot be improved by the Seller's offering or alternatively the customer does not have the money and cannot raise it, and in both of these instances a 'no sale' will result.

Quite often, customers are encouraged to change the way they do things as a part of a proposal to invest in the Seller's products or services, or both, to deliver measurable benefits to the customer's Profit & Loss account. This is called 're-engineering'.

The recipe is explained in terms of the ingredients necessary to create a Payback Sale together with the process that is used to provide readers with a description of what needs to be achieved, as distinct from how to do it. The 'how' relates to the ESPIRE® model which deals with the 'Matching' aspect of the Recipe. We know that when we show delegates how the Recipe works in a training programme, it provides them with a background road map of the journey they need to travel with a prospective customer to achieve a Payback Sale. The recipe simply states that if a customer can be shown that he has Needs that can be matched by Benefits with financial Values which outweigh the costs, they will usually go for it.

Obviously, customers develop their own processes and methodologies within their business which deliver the current results. There may well be much better ways in 'efficiency terms' of completing some of these processes, but managers and directors may not be aware of them. In these instances it could be said that, from a customer's perspective, they have no problems and therefore no Needs. The ingredients for a sale can be contained within two different scenarios; one where the customer or prospect takes the initiative because they have a Need, the other where the Seller takes the initiative because he or she knows where to look for Needs not yet recognised by the customer .

Examples:

Scenario One

> There are circumstances that occur with organisations which make them address an issue, and in these instances they may well approach potential suppliers. These instances outline the circumstances in which most sales occur. The customer approaches a supplier stating an interest. The supplier responds with a visit or contact usually followed by a demonstration and a quote against a buyer's stated need.

Scenario Two

> Payback Consultative Sellers learn through Benefit Analysis and experience how to recognise, through research, which prospective customers might well improve the efficiency of their current processes, and approach them using their Strong Benefit Statement, to arrange a meeting to conduct Situation Analysis. Many sales from new customers are created in this way, thereby providing Payback

Consultative Sellers with a methodology for growing their business on an ongoing basis over and above those sales written as a result of customers contacting them as in Scenario One. This methodology provides Payback Consultative Sellers with a very valuable and unique business development tool and separates Payback Consultative Selling from the traditional approach as outlined in Scenario One.

Payback Consultative Sellers may also be approached by customers who have stated an interest as in Scenario One. In these circumstances Payback Consultative Sellers would not provide a quotation, they would use the ESPIRE® model in exactly the same way as would be used approaching prospective customers in Scenario Two.

The sales process described in this publication shows clearly how both of these scenarios are dealt with in the same way. The big difference is that a traditional demonstration sale relies heavily on the customer initiating an interest generally referred to as a 'sales lead'. Payback Consultative Selling skills enable Sellers to have a much greater vision of which types of prospective customers should be approached in the knowledge that many of them can be encouraged to change the way they currently operate by investing in the Seller's offering.

Most readers will accept that following up a sales lead is quite different to making a 'cold call'. Traditional Sellers do not favour the cold call because of the high probability of a negative response.

The Recipe for a Sale uses the words 'Customer's Needs', but it can be seen from the two scenarios that some customers do have what they perceive as Needs and provide sales leads. However, many prospective customers have the ever-present and ongoing need to improve the efficiency and profitability of their businesses but do not always realise how this could be done. These types of prospects therefore, in their own opinion, do not have identified Needs. This explains why cold calling to leave a business card is a very expensive, speculative and negative sales approach. Payback Consultative Sellers have to create the Need in situations where they are approaching the customer in the absence of a 'lead'.

The Benefits and Value aspect of the Recipe has now been dealt with in detail and should be self explanatory. The Matching aspect is the methodology we use to bring Needs and Benefits together as a Payback Proposal (measured value add), which is encapsulated in the ESPIRE® model and this is dealt with in subsequent individual parts of this publication.

Key Notes from Part Three

1. The Recipe for a Sale outlines the circumstances that need to exist for a Payback Sale to take place.

2. The Recipe for a Sale is complete when the **Needs** of the customer are **Matched** by the **Benefits and Values** of the offering.

3. Customers sometimes think they know what they need but Payback Consultative Sellers know how to create Needs where previously they may not have appeared to exist.

4. Like a Recipe for a cake, the Recipe comprises two elements. The ingredients, which have to be the right ones in the right quantities, plus the process required to utilise the ingredients correctly to produce the required outcome.

5. Sometimes Sellers discover that the ingredients cannot be processed effectively to produce a sale. This can occur even when the Seller has perfected the Payback Consultative Selling methodology. This can also occur when it becomes clear that the application of the Seller's offering cannot improve the Customer's business from a financial standpoint. A 'no sale' can also result when the prospective customer simply does not have the money and is unable to raise it.

6. Customers sometimes have Needs which they identify themselves and therefore initiate a sales lead. Often customers end up buying a different solution than

they anticipated due to the discovery of new ideas or new products.

7. Payback Consultative Sellers can create the Recipe for a Sale through prospective customers who did not have identified Needs and who did not approach the Seller's organisation. These incremental sales represent a major benefit for the adoption of Payback Consultative Selling methodologies.

8. The Recipe provides Sellers with a 'road map' of the journey they need to complete with a prospective customer to create a Payback Sale using the ESPIRE® model.

PART FOUR - ESP PAYBACK CONSULTATIVE SELLING PROCESS - ESPIRE®

The ESP Payback Consultative Selling Process incorporates the ESPIRE® model, which is the face to face methodology specifically designed for Payback Consultative Selling.

Separate parts of this publication are dedicated to each stage, and each stage relates to each letter of the ESPIRE® acronym (model).

The Recipe for a Sale dealt with in Part Three represents the backdrop or road map to the sales process which means that the two main elements of the Recipe representing the ingredients and matching process are processed separately by using the six stages of the ESPIRE® model. The elements being (1) Customer Needs and Benefits and Values and (2) Matching

The following diagram (Figure 11) shows again the six stages of the model with a short form explanation of the activity that is completed against each stage, represented by each letter.

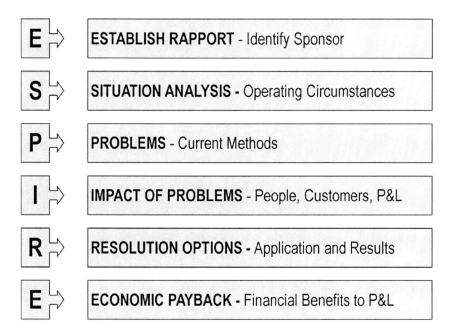

Figure11 - ESPIRE® Model

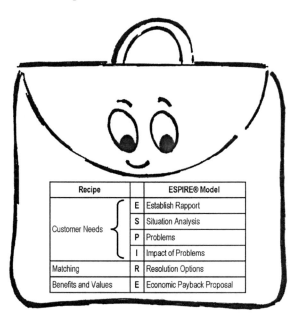

Figure 12 – The ESPIRE® model is the route map of the sales process.

Figure 12 shows you how the ESPIRE® model covers the elements of the Recipe for a Sale. It should be clear that not every prospect becomes a customer and it is worth repeating that the ESP Payback Consultative Selling methodology cannot guarantee that every prospect will have Needs or that, even if they do, they will recognise them or that you will be able to uncover them. Assuming that Needs are established, it may not be possible to demonstrate enough Value to get the prospect to buy. In other words, Sellers may not always be able to Match Needs with Benefits and Values by using the ESPIRE® Payback Consultative Selling model. What is guaranteed, however, is the following:

1. Sellers will always be able to have control of the process.

2. Sellers will be able to determine where they are in terms of likely success much more easily than by using any other method.

3. The ESP selling methodology always enables Sellers to be coming from a positive position of trying to help customers improve the business profitability which they will respect even if they do not buy.

4. This selling methodology always calls for a Payback Proposal (if the possibility exists) which avoids the problems associated with quotations awaiting decision.

   Note: *Readers will see in the section dealing with proposals why and how this statement is true.*

The following parts of this publication deal with each of the six stages of the ESPIRE® model in detail.

The Key Notes relating to this section summarise the relationship between the Recipe for a Sale and the ESPIRE® model.

Key Notes from Part Four

A Summary of the Relationship between the Recipe and the ESPIRE® Model

The ESPIRE® model is a process designed to establish if the ingredients for a sale exist with a prospect and, if they do, how to convince the prospect to buy using a Payback Proposal which may show a return on an investment or recovery of cost, partial or full.

The Recipe for a Sale contains two elements:

1. The Ingredients – Customer Needs and the Supplier's Benefits and Values

2. Matching - The Matching of the two ingredients is the process for making a successful sale. The Matching aspect of the Recipe for a Sale is incorporated in the ESPIRE® model which is used in the Payback Consultative Selling Process.

As mentioned in the Introduction, the process of learning is hampered by short term memory loss. The way to transfer new knowledge from short term memory to long term memory is by way of repetition so it is necessary to practice or revise. There is a lot to remember and practice in order to master the Payback Consultative Selling Process. If readers wish to experience the financial advantages of Payback Consultative Selling and reduce the stresses associated with achieving sales goals using traditional methods, the process must be learned and remembered thoroughly from beginning to end. The next page sets out a number of questions to represent a review of those areas covered so far. Test your knowledge by completing the review and checking your results by referring to the answers printed on the following page. Go for it!

Review of Parts One to Four

Review Questions

1. Why do Buyers say 'No' as detailed in the Introduction?

2. What is the definition of the word Benefit?

3. Name any two typical Benefits that deliver savings to users.

4. What are the three principal financial areas that businesses are seeking to improve?

5. What are the three connected components of Benefit Analysis?

6. Where do the questions for use during Situation Analysis originate?

7. What is the purpose of a Strong Benefit Statement?

8. What are the three areas of focus for Benefit Analysis relating to a typical company offering?

9. Where is the source of Value?

10. What is Value?

11. What is Payback Consultative Selling?

12. What are the elements of the Recipe for a Sale?

13. What are the six stages by letter only of the ESP model used in the Payback Consultative Selling Process?

Review Answers

1. *They cannot see a reason to say 'yes'.*

2. *What something 'does' and not what 'it is'.*

3. *Saving of time, money, energy, pain, life.*

4. *Revenues or sales, gross margin or profit, cost reduction.*

5. *Features, Advantages and Benefits.*

6. *The Benefit Analysis.*

7. *To motivate prospects to willingly participate with Situation Analysis.*

8. *The Products or Services, the Company, the Sales Person.*

9. *The Benefit Analysis.*

10. *The extent to which Benefits will produce financial gain.*

11. *Demonstrating where possible how the costs of an application are recovered, thereby creating an investment opportunity.*

12. *Two elements:*

    12.1. Ingredients = Needs plus Benefits and Values

    12.2. Matching = ESPIRE® model

13. *ESPIRE®.*

If you answered all the questions correctly, well done. If you did not, review the section of the book that deals with it.

PART FIVE - E - ESTABLISHING RAPPORT AND INDENTIFYING SPONSORS

Most sellers understand the importance of relationships. Good and enduring relationships are based on trust, rapport and credibility, and building new ones can take time.

We know that time is a valuable commodity for both sellers and buyers. In today's markets, getting new influential prospects to give us the necessary time to build a relationship is a major challenge. We therefore have to be smarter than ever before, both prior to and during visits with new contacts.

There are many books and publications written on the subject of strategic selling, many of which focus on the following:

1. Which new customers represent the ideal target for the benefits and values of our offering?

2. What is the buying process within the organisation?

3. Who are the budget holders, decision makers, influencers and potential sponsors?

    [**Note**: A sponsor is a person within an organisation who, once motivated to support our offering, helps us gain access to the real decision makers.]

4. How will the different aspects of the business and the people associated with these aspects benefit from our solution or offering?

Obtaining meaningful answers to all of the above questions represents an important aspect of strategic selling. All are subject to methodologies and processes to effectively establish the answers and it is well worth studying the recognised manuscripts written by experts in their field.

Different types of businesses are structured in different ways. Large organisations will inevitably contain various departments or divisions with a specific responsibility or focus as depicted in Figure 13. These departments have heads or managers responsible for them. These individuals may have influence over expenditure and be interested in different aspects of a product or service.

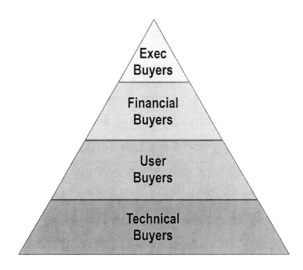

Figure 13 – Buying Influencers

At the back of this publication we have noted a number of books on various subjects which we recommend and among these readers can locate suitable references on strategic selling.

This section is dedicated to the first 'E' aspect of the ESPIRE® model which focuses on Establishing Rapport. Let us assume that the necessary pre-visit research has been completed and an appointment made with a decision maker within a prospective customer.

Readers will remember that the Strong Benefit Statement can be used when making appointments, given that the Benefit Statement should be evolved to convey to prospective customers that there are potentially profitable reasons why the prospect should agree to an appointment. The same Strong Benefit Statement should be re-used during the first 'E' stage of the ESPIRE® model, as previously mentioned, but as some time may have elapsed since an appointment was made the prospect may not remember the detail of your Strong Benefit Statement, so repeating it is exactly the right thing to do.

We have already mentioned that in some large organisations it may be necessary to see several people. The same process should be used with each person although, because their principal responsibilities and interests may be different, it may be important to focus on different benefits by asking different Lead Questions during the Situation Analysis. Any effective Payback Proposal therefore, to such an organisation, cannot be evolved until everyone concerned in the buying process has been seen. The proposal will focus on the benefits and values that can relate to the different aspects of the prospect's business.

During training programmes, we always emphasise that *'Everything we say or do when face to face with a prospect either moves us closer to or further away from any prospective business'*. This being so, it follows that everything we say and do 'counts' and needs to be deliberate rather than accidental.

Establishing rapport, therefore, is a very important aspect of the whole process. Prior to visiting the prospect, the Seller should have done their research and know quite a bit about the prospect's business already. The basic knowledge that builds rapport and shows the prospect that the necessary time and effort has been taken to research basic information is as follows:

1. How long the business has been established

2. Turnover and profit (accounts may be available from Companies House; Dun & Bradstreet; Mint, and Websites)

3. The prospective company's size compared to the market

4. Products and services

5. Method of distribution and marketing

6. Major competitors

7. Key executives and managers

This list is not exhaustive but research takes up valuable selling time so it is necessary to take a common sense view of what information is gathered. If the prospect has big potential, more time would be warranted on research than if the prospect is smaller. The art of working smart is to locate what we call 'low hanging fruit', if it exists, and focus on that first.

Let us go back to our imaginary appointment. Immediately the Seller is face to face with the prospect, the ESPIRE® model begins.

What follows is a detailed description of what the Seller does during the first 'E' stage and is followed by a brief description to aid memory.

E ESTABLISH RAPPORT – Identify Sponsors

Let us now break this open and track every aspect of what a Payback Consultative Seller needs to do upon meeting the prospect:

1. Traditional greeting, Seller's name and position.

2. Commence a pre-prepared preamble (about anything other than the business meeting purpose). Encourage the prospect to participate. The preamble should only take a few minutes to ensure the prospect feels comfortable and relaxed. This preamble also provides the Seller with an opportunity to decide if the atmosphere and circumstances are conducive to a sales conversation and that the prospect is able to give attention to the matter in hand. In the event that this proves not to be the case, the Seller can make another appointment, stating the Benefits of doing so to the prospect.

3. Deliver your Strong Benefit Statement ending with "We are not sure if we will be able to improve your profitability but may I be permitted to ask a few relevant questions to find out?". If your Benefit

Statement strikes a cord of interest with the prospect, they should be happy to cooperate with answering your 'Lead Questions' which you will already have prepared. Clearly, you may have more than a **few** questions to ask, but in the early stages of the meeting we do not want the prospect to imagine that they are in for a long drawn out boring time. If they become interested as the discussions ensue, they will be less focused on the time.

Immediately Sellers start to ask Lead Questions they are focusing on the operational circumstances of the prospect's business which we call Situation Analysis. This represents the next stage of the ESPIRE® model, as discussed in the following section.

PART SIX - S - SITUATION ANALYSIS – ANALYSING CUSTOMERS' OPERATING CIRCUMSTANCES

It is worth highlighting exactly where the ESPIRE® model fits into the whole Payback Consultative Selling Process. The following graph (Figure 14) illustrates the activities concerned with winning new business from new customers or new business from existing customers. As previously mentioned, some research is necessary prior to making visits, and some of these activities readers will be familiar with and are therefore not focused on in this book. The activities that need to be completed prior to making visits are:

- Prospecting (establishing details of customers that might buy)

- Making Appointments (accessing decision makers)

Figure 14 also shows all the activities that require successful completion from prospecting through to obtaining an order. All of these activities take 'time' and, therefore, one axis of the graph is the time and the other is the activity.

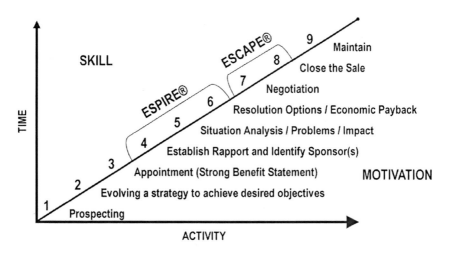

Figure 14 – ESP Payback Consultative Selling Process

At the end of Part 5 we stated that immediately the Seller commences with Lead Questions aimed at establishing the customer's current operating circumstances, Situation Analysis has been initiated. The 'S' of ESPIRE®.

In the event that the customer is well motivated to cooperate with the seller to answer the Situation Analysis questions (Lead Questions) the Seller should start to understand the customer's current operating circumstances.

To enable Sellers to establish circumstances that could be improved by the application of the seller's offering the next two letters of the ESPIRE® model after 'E' and 'S' are 'P' and 'I'.

'P' and 'I' stand for Problems and Impact and these are fully dealt with in Part Seven.

It is important to note and understand that the 'P' and 'I' represent an integral part of Situation Analysis, because if there are any problems and challenges which are currently causing negative impact on the business, then these Problems, with their Impact, represent part of the current situation.

Remember to ask open questions, one at a time. Listen to the answers. Sellers have two ears and one mouth and they should be utilised in that ratio.

It is therefore important that questions should be focused to see if the prospect has any problems judged against their ideals. In this context, the word 'problem' means any gap between where the customer's business is now in efficiency terms against where they would like to be. Remember that we are focusing on the financial aspects of the prospect's business. Here are some examples:

- They may be behind their sales plan/budget
- They may be struggling with margin
- They may be short on budgeted profit
- They may have people or operational problems
- Costs may be spiralling
- They could have cash flow problems

The next section shows us how to focus questions asked during Situation Analysis on the 'Problems' that might represent a GAP between where the prospect is and where they would like to be. In addition, we should also attempt to establish the cause for the gap and the extent of motivation on behalf of the buyer to close the gap.

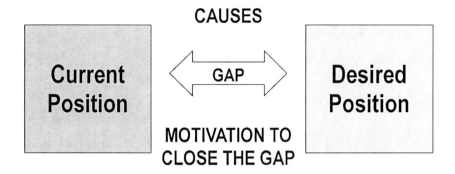

Figure 15 – The Gap

In summary, therefore, asking the Lead Questions from the Benefit Analysis during Situation Analysis is done purely to identify Problems or gaps and the Impact of those Problems and gaps on the business. In this way, Situation Analysis is not a standalone aspect of the process as it incorporates the Problem and Impact aspects.

PART SEVEN - P - PROBLEMS AND THEIR IMPACT

P PROBLEMS – Current Methods

It is a fact of life that every person on the planet develops habits and belief systems as the result of their experiences as they progress through life. People in business are no different. Some tend to operate their businesses in a way that they have always done it and are sometimes slow to change due to:

- Their habits (they always do it that way)

- Their beliefs (they believe that circumstances are not easy to change without risk and they are comfortable with what they know)

Payback Consultative Sellers need to be aware that, for many reasons, many organisations are inefficient in some form or other. It follows, therefore, that if a prospect is asked if they have any problems, they are more than likely to say no. The reason is as described. They have probably been using present methodologies or products or services for some time and they do not see this as a problem. Quite often a Payback Consultative Seller knows of a much better way of doing something with their products or services and often makes the wrong assumption that the customer would know the same. Here's the news! They do not! This is why a standard demonstration, showing what a product or service is and how it works, can be a risky and ineffective way of obtaining business.

You will recall the description of a Consultant. They are specialists or experts in their field which means that they identify how to do 'things' better. The first thing to do, just like Doctors is to find out how 'things' are being done now. Hence the function of Situation Analysis, i.e. ascertaining current operating circumstances. In relation to 'how things are being done', we mean processes of the business and the results of those processes relative to how they might be done with the Seller's products or services.

Identifying Problems, therefore, is the Payback Consultative Seller's role and not the prospect's. So the 'P' of ESPIRE® is there to remind you of what you are attempting to do during Situation Analysis.

The process so far dealt with is:

E   ESTABLISH RAPPORT

S   SITUATION ANALYSIS

P   PROBLEMS

Just to remind you, the type of problems you are looking for, whilst conducting Situation Analysis, are any gaps that exist between where the prospect's business is now, against where they would like it to be. These gaps might be financial, physical, or strategic. It may be that you now need to review the structure of your Lead Questions to ensure that they focus on uncovering any gaps or problems. Do not be shy about making notes of customers' answers or of using notes as a prompt to ask your pre-prepared questions. If you find a gap or a problem, do not fall into the trap of discussing at that point how you might be able to solve it. Indeed, DO NOT MAKE ANY PROPOSITIONS until you have completely finished conducting full Situation Analysis. Ask all the Lead Questions relative to all the Benefits which you think are relevant.

If and when you find gaps or problems, the next stage is to ascertain how significant they are in terms of to what extent they might be inhibiting the efficiency of the business. By 'efficiency', we mean maximising return on the assets. The bigger the problem, the easier the sale!

Remember that the purpose of Payback Consultative Selling is to be able to make a Payback Proposal.

Value is the extent to which a business might be improved financially when the Benefits of the offering are applied to a business.

These two points are being repeated here because we need to quantify in financial terms the extent of any gaps or problems established through our questions. The 'I' of ESPIRE® means the 'impact' of any problems on the business in measurable financial terms. When attempting to identify the problems or gaps, do so knowing that the size of the Impact of the problems is a critical aspect of Situation Analysis. Hence, the ESPIRE® acronym was designed with the Problems and their Impact being highlighted separately. So, when you have identified a Problem, visualise in your mind the next aspect to investigate.

I IMPACT OF PROBLEMS - People, Customers, P&L

Sometimes you will identify an operational problem that occurred in the past but the prospect is not able to put a financial figure to it. In these instances try to agree assumptive numbers with the prospect so that they can be used and substantiated in the building of an economic Payback Proposal. It is important to know ballpark figures so that if your solution or offering can save all or part of this money, you need to be able to show what it is; factual and/or assumed.

It is critical that readers understand this aspect of the process, reading it several times if necessary, because if you are unable to show how your offering can save all or part of the costs sustained as the result of the problem, you are unable to show the value of your offering as a Payback Proposal.

In summary, the Situation Analysis aspect of the sales process is concerned with asking Lead Questions from the Benefit Analysis that are geared to locate gaps or problems with the functions and operations of the prospect's business. If any gaps or problems are located, the Seller needs to quantify the extent of those problems in financial terms, particularly when the Seller knows that the problems could be negated, or at least partially mitigated, by the application of their offering. In this regard, the 'S', 'P' and 'I' aspects of the sales process work together.

Figure 16 – Sellers establish Problems and their Impact during Situation Analysis

As said previously, selling is very much about common sense and not rocket science. There are no 'rabbits to pull out of hats' or 'magic wands' encapsulated in Payback Consultative Selling. Either an opportunity exists or it does not. Payback Consultative Selling, when conducted properly, will always expose an opportunity if one exists or, in some instances, create an opportunity due to knowledge the Seller has but the prospect does not.

Demonstration selling in itself cannot identify opportunity. Establishing an opportunity in this context means that problems against the ideal have been identified and the impact or extent of them has been established financially. Establishing an opportunity or establishing the opposite is exactly the function and purpose of the first four parts of the **ESPIRE®** model:

E   ESTABLISH RAPPORT

S   SITUATION ANALYSIS

P   PROBLEMS

I   IMPACT OF PROBLEMS ON BUSINESS

Let us imagine two opposite outcomes from a consultative sales visit:

- Outcome 1
  A measurable opportunity DOES NOT exist
- Outcome 2
  A measurable opportunity DOES exist

Both of these outcomes are positive for the following reasons:

Outcome 1 – No Proposal. This is positive because you will not need to spend any more time and effort on the account until the circumstances change. Demonstration and quote selling take no less time in the initial stages but, because the extent of any opportunity is unknown, it is usual for considerable costly follow up activity to take place to chase up quotations in an attempt to close them, but with no real levers to use to motivate the prospect to take positive action.

Outcome 2 – An Opportunity. The reasons for this being a positive outcome are clear even though no sale has yet taken place. The next stage of the ESPIRE® model will provide you with a much better chance to convert the opportunity into a sale because you can offset the cost of your offering by showing savings or earnings on areas of problems which the customer has identified with you, hence the word 'Payback' is used in connection with this type of approach.

It should be reiterated at this point that in some instances you may not be able to identify the cost of Problems as an Impact, but with a little help from the prospect they can be estimated and used as an assumptive cost.

Before we continue with the 'R' stage of the ESPIRE® model, which is covered in the next part, we have again created a review enabling you to judge what knowledge you have been able to absorb and show you which aspects might need some revision.

Review of Parts Five to Seven

Review Questions

1. Provide 3 examples of information that pre-visit research could reveal.

2. What does the first 'E' of ESPIRE® stand for?

3. What is another way of describing problems in the ESPIRE® model?

4. Name three principal areas of P&L that should be probed during Situation Analysis?

5. What does the 'S' of ESPIRE® stand for?

6. What two character traits do humans have that cloud their need to change?

7. What does the 'I' of ESPIRE® stand for?

8. What is it that we really want to know relating to the impact of a problem?

9. What is the 'good news' associated with establishing that an opportunity does not exist?

Review Answers

1. How long established, turnover, profit, size, product and services, method of distribution/marketing, major competition.

2. Establish rapport.

3. Gaps between actual and desired status.

4. Sales revenues – gross margin – running costs.

5. Situation Analysis.

6. Habits and beliefs.

7. Impact.

8. The associated costs.

9. The saving of follow up time and associated costs

PART EIGHT - R - RESOLUTION OPTIONS

Many sales people will be familiar with the expression 'Solution to Problems'. The Payback Consultative Selling Process is not entirely removed from this concept. The objective of the ESP sales methodology is for the Seller to identify what they perceive to be problems against objectives and then qualify the financial impact of those problems, with the goal being to resolve them by way of an economic Payback Proposal.

'Resolution Options' means what options does a seller have to resolve the Problems and their Impact identified during Situation Analysis. The Seller will have either identified gaps / problems or not.

The way forward from this point is the subject of this section and assumes there is a sales opportunity to address the needs identified with a prospect. Resolution Options requires no input at this point from the prospect.

Each separate aspect of the ESPIRE® model forms a navigation system enabling the sales person to know where they are at any point and, more importantly, what to do next. The letters within the acronym ESPIRE® are designed for you to be able to visualise them one at a time and conduct the activity for each as well as you are able, and then move on to the next almost regardless of the outcome. Many traditional sales people are so anxious to get an order that they are continually pressing a prospect in this direction which can feel uncomfortable for both parties. It is for this reason that sales people are not generally appreciated by customers and prospects.

Figure 17 - High pressure selling is uncomfortable for Sellers and Buyers

Payback Consultative Selling, as previously mentioned, is about improving a customer's business if it is at all possible. In the event that a Seller has not been able to identify any gaps or problems to close by the application of their offerings, then clearly there is no sale. If the prospect has been properly evaluated during the research aspect of prospecting then, in the majority of cases, Situation Analysis will reveal opportunities. During the 'Impact' aspect of the ESPIRE® model, you will have attempted to establish the cost of any identified problems, and you will need this information to establish the basis of a proposition. Establishing the basis of a proposition is clearly a 'thinking and considering' activity that takes place during the Resolution Option phase of ESPIRE®.

R RESOLUTION OPTIONS – Application & Results

In the event that Sellers have not identified any gaps or problems during the Situation Analysis phase of the model, the Impact aspect does not apply. As there would be no options to resolve either non existent or non identified problems in these instances, the Seller should tell the prospect, having thanked them for their time, that you are unable to see how they can improve profitability. At this juncture, you will recall that we have recommended that in your Strong Benefit Statement you make the point that you need to ask some questions and receive answers before you will know if you can improve profitability. If, having asked the relevant questions, you are not able to see how you could improve profitability, telling the prospect that this is the position should not in any way upset them, particularly given the structure of your opening statement.

The Resolution Options stage of the ESPIRE® model is, therefore, about the Seller considering how two elements of a scenario can be matched together to create financial improvement for the prospect's business. The two elements to consider are:

- Can the benefits of the Seller's offering be applied to the prospect's operating circumstances to measurably make a positive difference?

- Has the Seller been able to identify the potential values of the benefits having conducted thorough Situation Analysis?

You will recall from Part Three that these elements represent the Recipe for a Sale.

We have already dealt with how to deal with a scenario where the answer to the above two elements is NO. If the answer is YES then the basis of a proposal exists. In either event, you should summarise your findings when you have completed the Situation Analysis.

In the event of positive findings, i.e. you believe that the basis of a Payback Proposal exists, you have a choice regarding the timings and logistics for conducting the Resolution Options aspect of the model.

Your options are as follows:

1. Advise the prospect that you want to return to your offices to consider how to construct and calculate the basis of a Payback Proposal and then compile it for presentation.

2. Present your Payback Proposal there and then.

These options vary according to the complexity of the application of your offering, the competitive context, and the extent to which financial calculations need to be made. There will be more about this in the next section. In short, if the cost of your application runs into thousands, and the application of products or services or both is more than simple, or if re-engineering of any processes are required, a formal

Payback Proposal document should be constructed which will inevitably mean the necessity for production time. It is usual in Payback Consultative Selling that a further visit is required due to the necessity to produce a Payback Proposal document. A follow up visit also provides the Seller with an opportunity to demonstrate the Values of the proposal as a forerunner to closing the sale.

You will no doubt by now understand that unless you have a very deep knowledge of the benefits and potential values of your offering, together with the skill to conduct effectively a comprehensive Situation Analysis with whomever needs to be seen to ascertain the potential values of the benefits, Resolution Options cannot be developed. In a like manner to a Doctor, if they are unable to diagnose what is making a patient unwell, they would not be able to prescribe a cure. Similarly if they were able to diagnose what was wrong with the patient, but did not have sufficient knowledge about 'cures', an effective prescription would be equally impossible.

In order for Payback Consultative Selling to work effectively, the Seller needs to acquire the necessary skill to diagnose and prescribe successfully. They also need to organise their time so that they have the capacity to carry out the function with sufficient new prospects to build revenues on an organised basis. Thirdly, they need to be well motivated to do it. If you are a sales manager, you need to create these three components of skill, time and motivation within your sales teams by measuring their effectiveness in these areas and closing any identified gaps by coaching and training. ESP Sales Management Training focuses on these areas as a methodology for using the Natural Law of Cause and Effect to deliver measurable outcomes.

A review of this section follows before the final stage of the ESPIRE® model, which deals with the last 'E' - Economic Payback Proposal.

Review of Part Eight

Review Questions

1. How would a prospect contribute whilst the Seller completes the activity associated with the Resolution Options aspect of the ESPIRE® model?

2. What should Sellers do when they have completed Situation Analysis?

3. What should Sellers do if, during Situation Analysis, they are unable to establish how an offering might improve the customer's business by the application of your offering?

4. What is the purpose of conducting Situation Analysis?

5. What is another way of describing the kind of problems Sellers are looking for whilst conducting Situation Analysis?

6. When Sellers discover a Problem, or a gap, what is it they next need to know about such Problems?

7. What two skills or areas of knowledge does a Doctor need in order to cure a patient's illness?

8. What three competencies of a Seller should Sales Managers be principally concerned with?

Review Answers

1. None. It is purely an activity of the Seller.

2. Summarise the findings of the Situation Analysis to the prospect.

3. Tell the prospect.

4. To ascertain the potential values of the benefits of the Seller's offering.

5. The gaps between where the prospect's business is in performance terms against where the prospect would like it to be.

6. The Impact of the Problem on the business or the people and, particularly, any associated costs.

7. Skills or knowledge of a Doctor:

   7.1. To be able to accurately complete a diagnosis of the patient's problem.

   7.2. To know what the cure is and how to prescribe it.

8. Skill, Time Management, and Motivation.

If you were unable to answer all of these questions, do not be surprised as the required information has not been transferred to long term memory. Review previous sections of the book as necessary.

PART NINE - ECONOMIC PAYBACK PROPOSALS

An important key aspect of Payback Consultative Selling is to be in a position, where possible, to demonstrate value prior to quoting price. You will recall from the Introduction that prospects see price as a cost, which has a negative effect on their P&L account. Payback means that customers can see how they may recover the costs and ideally generate a profit on those costs. Value and Payback can only be demonstrated if the Seller is able to apply the Economic Benefits to the Buyer's business in such a way as to generate either a partial cost recovery, full recovery or even better a profit return on the cost of the Seller's offering.

Figure 18 – Payback Proposals ideally cost less than the Customer gets back

The previous Book Parts have been given over to the processes that the Seller needs to follow to ascertain if Value and Payback can be demonstrated and, if so, how. The 'how' of showing prospects the application of the Seller's offering to show a return on the costs and, if possible, to what extent in measurable financial terms, is the subject of the last letter 'E' of the ESPIRE® model which stands for

E ECONOMIC PAYBACK - Financial Benefits to P&L

At this juncture, it is important to make the point that 'Payback' can be demonstrated in two ways as follows:

- Showing prospects what aspects of their P&L will be improved by accepting a proposal to procure the Seller's offering. Remember, basically there are only three ways a P&L can be affected and these are income (sales) or gross margin or cost reduction or a combination. Sellers should demonstrate actual figures where they can, and these figures would be taken from information gleaned during Situation Analysis in the area of Problems and the Impact in financial terms of identified problems on the business.

- The other way of doing it is more sophisticated and uses standard accountancy measures of Economic Value Add (EVA) known as ROI (Return on Investment). A section at the end of this section is given over to this formal aspect of measurable Value Add.

In both cases, the economic component of a proposal shows 'Payback', i.e. how the cost is partially or fully recovered, and whether a profit is generated over and above the initial cost together with the time frame for payback to be realised.

For the purposes of dealing with proposals, it is sufficient to understand that the construction of a Payback Proposal is the same whatever method is used. The only difference is in the way in which financial benefits are presented in the proposal, i.e. formally (ROI) or informally (P&L improvement).

There are a number of good reasons for producing a written Payback Proposal outside those related to a method of showing prospects how the application of the Seller's offering impacts positively on their P&L. These additional reasons are:

1. In some cases your sponsor or contact may need to convince others of the benefits of investing in the proposal. This could be the Board or other influencers. Clearly, Sellers should use their best endeavours to directly sell to any identified influencers, as Sellers are trained to sell benefits and payback, whereas influencers will only usually want to look at costs. Sometimes, however, for a number of reasons, it may not be possible for Sellers to sell directly to everyone involved in the buying process. It is for this reason that a documented Payback Proposal has additional advantages as it can be sent by your prospect or sponsor to additional people.

2. A documented proposal necessitates careful preparation and can contain well thought out arguments that are described with clarity to demonstrate the best argument for the purchase. Sellers doing this face to face, unless using a formal presentation, will struggle to communicate the financial benefits effectively.

3. Sellers can use a documented proposal to show their own management the exact status of any live prospect in the closing stages of a sale.

It is now necessary to show you the recommended contents of a Payback Proposal, and the sections are as follows:

- An Executive Summary
- A Summary of the Customer's Situation/Needs
  - Problems – Impact - Gap
- A Description of the proposed Application of Products/Services
- Business Case including Economic Benefits (Payback) and ROI Measures if calculable
- Details of any Non-Economic Benefits
- Pricing or Leasing/Rental Rates
- Contract/Terms and Conditions

An overview of each section will enable readers to understand their construction and the content detail as well as the purpose of each section. The format of the completed proposal can take various forms dependent upon the intended method of delivery of the document, i.e. email, post or by hand. ESP believes very strongly that Sellers should present the contents of a proposal directly to Decision Makers in order to have maximum influence and control over the outcome. It is whilst demonstrating the Benefits in financial Payback form that the Seller has the maximum opportunity to persuade a prospect to accept the proposal. Persuading is a key role of Sellers. Clearly, therefore, Sellers need to decide upon the ideal format for the proposal to cater for the requirements of both the Seller and the Buyer. It is usual to compose a covering letter or email to accompany the proposal, whatever means is being used to deliver it, which enables the Seller to communicate any relevant information relating to the proposal.

Figure 19 – A Payback Proposal can have various formats

The Executive Summary

Purpose

The Summary is a précis of the key points of the whole proposal. Busy executives who can influence a purchase may be reluctant to read a whole proposal and may seek to find what they think are the relevant points, particularly the price. A Summary enables the Seller to demonstrate benefits and values in a short form format. If an influencer or even a decision maker takes interest as the result of the Summary, they may be motivated to look at the detail in the rest of the document. The Summary should contain numerical calculations of Value where possible for the obvious reason that executives are usually strongly focused on quantative financial performance.

You will recall that an earlier reference was made to demonstration selling culminating in quotations accompanied by technical specifications or brochures. Most businesses now exercise tight controls over capital expenditure, so reference to higher authority by any level in an organisation is now commonplace. Senior executives being asked to review a quote and a technical specification is one of the main reasons why this type of offer sits in 'awaiting decision status'. We have also said that Buyers will say 'No' unless they can think of a reason for saying 'Yes'.

Quotes awaiting action are often the subject of the 'No' response. An executive summary quoting financial benefits of a purchase attempts to provide the reason for the reader to say 'Yes'. The more compelling the financial argument, the more compelled executives are to say 'Yes'. Executives are spending money every day in all sorts of areas in an attempt to create profits. An Executive Summary sets out to show them why spending the money on your proposal makes good business sense.

Summary of Customer Situation / Needs

The title of this section of the proposal is almost self-explanatory. It is a summary, in your opinion, of the operating circumstances that you established during the Situation Analysis aspect of the ESPIRE® model. You will recall that, at the end of your Situation Analysis, to identify problems or gaps against ideals and the financial impact of them, you should verbally summarise your findings to the prospect at that time.

The written Summary of the Customer Situation follows the same flavour as your verbal summary but is carefully constructed to ensure that the prospect, or any other reader of the document, can clearly picture the present situation. Highlight any problems or gaps identified, together with the impact that these problems are having on the business either from a people or operational standpoint. Include any financial impact as accurately as possible as this will be the focus of your solutions to rectify these issues by the application of your offering.

The Needs aspect of the sub-title of this section does not relate to what the prospect thinks they 'need'. Needs in this instance refer to what you, the Seller, identify as issues that need to be resolved for the financial improvement of the business. Do not embellish or exaggerate the circumstances as it is not necessary and we do not want prospects to see a proposal as a sales pitch in the traditional 'overselling' sense.

Description of Product/Service Application

In this section, it is necessary to portray the application of the offering in terms of how it delivers benefits, and / or values with Payback, as well as a description of the products or services. The focus therefore is to outline how your offering should be utilised in the business to deliver financial values. Some products can be customised via various options in order to operate in a specific manner to deliver advantages over the existing methods. We know, of course, that Advantages can deliver Benefits and Benefits can be translated into Financial Values.

Business Case

The word 'case' means an argument to substantiate a view. In law, the expression 'The Case' for either the defendant or the accused means the argument or rationale substantiating their plea or position. A Business Case is therefore an argument or rationale behind a business proposition.

Earlier in this section we have explained the contents and format of proposals that demonstrate Payback. These proposals could also be described as Business Cases.

Readers will know that investment/expenditure budgets do not now usually exist as a matter of right. Cash is tight and its expenditure usually has to be justified. Directors now either approve budgets for a project ahead of reviewing actual proposals or approve expenditure of any consequence at the proposal stage.

Large corporate organisations will set minimum levels of expected return on any investment and this will be one of the tests that will be applied to an expenditure proposal. This minimum level is commonly known in accounting as the 'Hurdle Rate'.

Accountants are often asked to review large expenditure proposals and to translate them into a common set of measures so that directors can compare and assess investment or expenditure proposals on a like for like basis. These standard accountancy measures are commonly used in most businesses and are known as ROI measures (Return on Investment).

It is not the intention in this publication to go too deep with this subject but to provide an overview for the purposes of understanding how Payback Proposals fit into the ROI arena.

This section on Business Cases deals with the measures of ROI and why they are used. We should point out that there are complexities associated with calculating ROI measures accurately. When ROI measures are used they would form the principal aspect of a Payback Proposal.

In order to be able to calculate ROI, specific information must be obtained from the customer or assumptions agreed and this in itself can represent a considerable challenge dependent upon the position, knowledge and cooperation of the contact being sold to.

It is for these reasons that ROI measures and their calculation form the advanced level of Payback Consultative Selling.

ROI Measures

There are three measures for ROI, all of which are interrelated and should all be calculated in a majority of instances:

- **Payback (Time)** – Months

    - Payback (Time) is a simple measure, usually related to cash flow, of the time taken to recover any investment or expenditure in terms of years or months. This is an uncomplicated measure but does not take any account of risk, ROI, interest rates or anything else that key decision makers usually require.

- **Net Present Value (NPV)** - £/$/€

    - NPV is an investment appraisal technique that takes the minimum investment return (hurdle rate) required by companies and applies this percentage rate to the projected cash inflows and outflows for a project. This method therefore takes into account the time value of money. The resultant figure is either positive or negative. A positive NPV represents a surplus after recovering an investment measured in currency at today's money values. A surplus NPV usually leads to project or expenditure acceptance whereas a negative number will normally lead to rejection. Sometimes a return cannot always be expected or calculated on certain cost items, e.g. forklift trucks, and in this example a reduction in operating costs may justify switching expenditure to another supplier.

- **Internal Rate of Return (IRR)** - %

    - Companies appraise investments by comparing the benefits against the costs, and discounting these cash flows with reference to time. The IRR is the discount rate that, when applied to the cash outflows and inflows, delivers a project NPV of zero. This is therefore the actual percentage (%) return per annum on the funds used for the investment. A high IRR shows a very profitable project whereas a low IRR delivers lower percentage returns.

Directors or a Decision Making Unit (DMU) reviewing a Business Case which contains supported ROI calculations can clearly and easily assess the following:

1. How long it will take before they get the cost of their investment back.

2. How much money they would get back, taking several factors into account:

    2.1.   The ramp up or down of income resulting from the investment

    2.2.   The fact that money devalues over time

    2.3.   The risk of tying capital (cash) up in the project – probability of success

    2.4.   The sensitivity and accuracy of the data in estimating the cash inflows

There are often competing projects and expenditures within companies all requiring approval. The IRR could be used to compare annual rates of return for each expenditure request with the company's own internal minimum return expectations.

Calculating ROI Measures

ESP recommends a software tool developed and licensed by Shark Finesse Ltd. (www.sharkfinesse.com) as their offering enables customers to procure a bespoke and fully customised ROI calculation business tool for their market. Shark Finesse provides a range of ROI sales tools to increase and accelerate customer spend, and radically improve sales-team efficiency.

The key features, as reproduced from their website home page, are as follows:

- The core offering is a standalone software product for use by sales-teams in front of the customer without any need for external consultants.

- This ROI solution was designed and built using feedback from sales-teams and includes unique features introduced from the field.

- It enhances all existing sales and technical processes that have historically failed to address the vital economic question of "Why should I spend more money today?"

- The software identifies economic benefits, automates the calculation of three key ROI measures, and produces a concise board report for presentation and budget approval.

Details of Non-Economic Benefits

Instances arise whereby the application of an offering does deliver benefits, either to the business itself or to specific individuals, but these benefits cannot be measured in financial terms. Three examples of this type of benefit are:

- Peace of mind

- Ease of use

- Enhanced brand recognition

Sellers need to consider to what extent the inclusion of any non-economic benefits will add leverage to the proposal. Where Sellers feel that they should be mentioned then they should be dealt with separately from measurable benefits detailed in the Executive Summary and the Application of Products and Services.

Pricing or Leasing/Rental Rates

The positioning of Price in any sales process, either oral or written, is critical to the outcome. Payback Consultative Sellers know that Buyers will consider any price 'too high' unless they can see value. For this reason, this section dealing with Price in the Proposal appears well below those sections dealing with Benefits and Values. The positioning of price should be done so that it is shown as an investment rather than a cost. In the event that the normal price has been discounted due to the size of the potential business or the importance of the prospect's business then such discounting and the circumstances should be explained in this section.

Contract/Terms and Conditions

Most organisations produce printed terms and conditions for trading which deal with payment terms, warranties and the like. Similarly, they will have standard order forms or, in the case of more complex transactions, there may be a customised legal contract. All of these documents can be included in this section at the end of the Proposal.

Review of Part Nine

1. It is important to demonstrate value before communicating price. Payback Proposals should be constructed specifically to facilitate this.

2. Demonstrating a return on the cost presents the price as an investment.

3. There are three main components to a profit and loss account (P&L) and these are:

   3.1. Sales – Revenue – Income

   3.2. Gross Margin: the difference between the cost of either making/producing goods or services or and the selling price

   3.3. The Costs associated with running the business

4. There are two ways to demonstrate Value:

   4.1. Showing the actual monetary value of savings or revenues

   4.2. Using the standard accountancy measures of ROI = NPV, Payback, IRR %

5. Written proposals provide a controlled method of communicating values to third parties who may be involved in the buying process.

6. Sellers can use a written proposal to convince individuals within the customer's organisation of the Benefits and Values, but Sellers can also use them to show individuals within the Seller's organisation the status of a prospective sale.

PART TEN - DEMONSTRATING PAYBACK TO CLOSE SALES

Since professional selling began, 'closing the sale' has been a major focus of trainers and training schools. Many techniques have been evolved and used. The fact is, unless the prospect arrives at a mental position of 'Desire', closing the sale is almost impossible outside of using some other inducement leading to fear or personal gain, causing the Buyer to cooperate. Closing the sale is one thing, closing it without excessive price reduction is another. Today's markets are very price sensitive and often Sellers find themselves drawn into a price discussion well before any 'solutions to problems', or Benefits, have been discussed. Many of ESP's customers are saying that invitations to tender via the Internet are becoming prevalent. Any response by Sellers to discuss or quote a price remote from Benefits and Values cannot be described as selling by ESP's definition as there is no basis for persuasion.

The cost of sales resources has already been mentioned and companies have to decide what the role and purpose of sales resources are. Economically, they have to be able to generate sufficient margin on sales to generate a return on not just the operating cost of the company, but also the capital employed in the company. Quoting low prices, however and whenever it is done, without showing Value, is unlikely to fund the Seller's costs. If an organisation decides that it needs to be in the market where customers insist on receiving quotes in isolation to any other sales activity, it also needs to decide how it will recover the cost of that response, and the pricing that will be used. It is not economically possible to price products and services at the same level for marketing via the Internet or mail order, as would be the case when using personal selling. Within the introduction to this publication, we have highlighted the challenges associated with trading using a sales team in competitive markets in that, if the sales team becomes a mobile catalogue or human quoting machine, even with technical or specialist expertise, volume becomes the focus, and hope, rather than control, becomes the backdrop to the strategy. Being able to demonstrate Value and Payback, therefore, has three main Benefits for Sellers:

1. Demonstrating Value and Payback helps build desire to facilitate closing a sale.

2. Demonstrating Value and Payback creates less focus on the price due to the investment opportunity.

3. Only professional consultative sellers can demonstrate Value as catalogues and the internet cannot

Closing sales using the ESP Payback Consultative Selling methodology becomes an automatic function making it what used to be described as the Assumptive Close. Readers will understand from the ESPIRE® model that, if commercial buyers can see and believe that they will get more money back from a purchase than they pay out initially, it almost becomes what is called in modern parlance a 'no brainer'. At the risk of repeating this yet again, it is not every prospect that will be the source of an order resulting from a Payback Proposal. Payback Consultative Sellers, as they develop and perfect the ESPIRE® model, become more adept at identifying likely positive prospects based on easy recognition of the types of operation that can be financially improved by the application of the Seller's offering. Closing using the Payback Consultative Selling Process, therefore, is reliant upon being able to produce a Payback Proposal, meaning that the Seller is able to complete the 'R' and 'E' of the ESPIRE® model and that a resolution option does exist with measurable positive financial values.

Figure 20 – Closing Sales with a Payback Proposal creates desire

Payback Proposals will clearly vary in respect of the financial extent to which an investment in the purchase will create return. Part Nine deals with how a return on an investment is measured in terms of how much money is generated or saved and over what period of time. The bigger the return over the shortest time, the easier it becomes for the Seller to close the sale.

As detailed in Part Nine, the last letter of the ESPIRE® model, 'E', stands for 'Economic Payback' and can only occur when the Seller has a proposal to make within 'Resolution Options' of the ESPIRE® model.

Closing sales, therefore, is purely a mechanism by the Seller of demonstrating to Buyers or, put another way, 'showing' Buyers, how the application of the offering to their current operating circumstances generates a return and the extent of that return in measurable financial terms. Once the prospect accepts and understands the calculation of the return on the cost, it may be necessary for the Seller to prove that the application will work. Proving to a decision maker that a proposed application will deliver the Benefits and Values is quite a separate activity and is outside of the ESPIRE® model. However, in view of the importance of the necessity to provide proof in some instances, it is dealt with at this point.

Let us assume two scenarios, both based on a proposal showing a positive return on the cost of an offering:

SCENARIO 1

The Buyer accepts the calculation of the proposal and does not require proof that the application will work. The Seller should calculate the return per day, based on the number of working days in the customer's year. Some calculations of return will take time to take effect and, therefore, the annual returns may ramp up or down. In these cases, Sellers should do the calculations over several years and, again, divided by the additional working days. The reason that Sellers do this is to show Buyers how delaying the buying decision is actually costing potential profit. This approach represents a very powerful commercial argument for 'going ahead' with the minimum of delay.

SCENARIO 2

The Buyer accepts the calculations of the proposal but does require proof that the application will work in their particular operating circumstances. In these instances, Sellers have options as follows:

1. The Buyer could be referred to a reference site where a current customer experiencing positive results from a similar application is happy to share their experience with a new customer.

2. The Seller could set up a physical demonstration of the application either at the Buyer's location or at the Seller's location, to show how the application improves performance.

3. The Seller could arrange for the prospect to experience a trial. In these instances, the Seller should carefully construct measurable criteria with the Buyer in advance that demonstrate the extent of the success of the trial. Ideally, the Seller should pre-agree with the Buyer that when the measurable criteria are achieved, an order will be placed. It is also important that, where necessary, Buyers are trained in how to use any equipment forming part of the application. It is important that the expectations of Buyers be clearly identified and that they are not left to decide the criteria themselves for obvious reasons.

It can be understood from this section that closing sales using the ESPIRE® model becomes much easier and much more controlled than attempting to close using traditional demonstration and quote type selling. The reason is clear. If a Seller using Payback Consultative Selling is able to evolve a Payback Proposal with value add, that proposal can be used to create 'Desire' with the Buyer. As previously mentioned, closing without 'Desire' is practically impossible and the process of attempting this using the 'demonstration and quote' method is costly and relies heavily on the Buyer calculating for themselves if they should go ahead. Remember, if Buyers cannot find a reason to say "Yes", they will say "No". This explains why conversion rates are low using the 'demonstration and quote' method. Conversion rates using the Payback Consultative Selling methodology are proven to be much higher. ESP enjoys a conversion rate in excess of 90% when submitting Payback Proposals for training and consultancy services.

Many organisations today are very heavily reliant upon the conversion of enough tenders, or quotes, to generate sufficient margin to create a viable profit on their overall trading. Many such organisations do not have an insight or knowledge of the Payback Consultative Selling methodology and, therefore, have to focus on continually increasing activity to generate more leads and higher conversion rates. This approach to business relies heavily on market trends for growth. Readers who perfect the sales process as outlined in this publication will arm themselves with a methodology of delivering controlled levels of revenues, margin, and growth, thereby differentiating themselves from the many organisations still struggling using traditional selling methods.

To provide readers with an example of the difference between demonstration selling and Payback Consultative Selling, the following scenario is used to illustrate the point. The scenario is created around a Golf Professional (Pro), who has been requested by the club retaining him to promote and sell membership to guests paying green fees. The scenario demonstrates how the whole ESPIRE® model is used. We will explain what 'green fees' are for anyone not familiar with golf in terms of fees. Private clubs will usually offer a number of facilities including access to the golf course for an annual membership fee. Most of these clubs know that casual players might not deem it worthwhile to pay an annual membership fee for occasional access and offer a facility for 'pay and play' called a 'green fee'.

Golf Professionals are employed by their club to act as the specialist or expert in the game and its rules. The Pro will often run the shop, provide lessons, etc. and, in large clubs, they will have an assistant to fulfil the functions enabling the Head Professional to attend and play at professional events.

Back to the scenario. It will be necessary to invent some aspects which are as follows:

1. The annual membership fee is say £1000, with no joining fee, per person.

2. The green fee will be £30 per person to play a round of 18 holes during the weekday only. Non-members are not permitted to play at weekends in this scenario.

So how might a Golf Pro go about selling annual memberships to green fee paying guests assuming that he has no formal sales experience or sales training? A Golf Pro would understand, however, the Features and Advantages of membership and could verbalise them.

Let us set the scene for the sales pitch. A casual visitor arrives at the golf shop during a week day to pay a green fee and play a round of eighteen holes. The visitor waits for the Golf Pro to finish serving another person with some balls and tees.

The Pro says: "Good morning, how can I help you?" The visitor expresses his wish to play and enquires regarding the cost of the green fee. The Golf Pro responds with the cost of £30 and then follows up with "Perhaps you should consider paying an annual membership which provides a number of benefits. You can play at any time seven days a week as often as you like. You can book a 'tee time' and walk straight onto the course, no need to report to the 'Pro Shop'. You can enter competitions and events; qualify for an official handicap enabling you to play on courses that will only facilitate handicapped players. You will have full access to the club house and enjoy a good social life, all for just £1000 per annum." This type of 'show and tell' approach to selling is what ESP calls 'demonstration and quote' selling.

The visitor now processes this information in their mind in order to respond. Some might agree to join as the result of that sales pitch and, if they do agree to join, they will have calculated that the offer is worthwhile by their judgement, however they might make that judgement. It can be seen from this example that the buyer (in this case the guest) is left to calculate for themselves the Benefits of joining. Payback Consultative Sellers do not allow buyers to calculate anything as the consultative seller does it for them. This is the major difference between demonstration selling and Payback Consultative Selling.

Let us now consider how the sales process to sell annual membership would be used if the Pro had been ESP trained in Payback Consultative Selling using the ESPIRE® model. Remember that the word 'selling' means 'convincing', which is a pro-active process for the Seller.

Readers will recall from Part One that there are three preparation exercises to complete before conducting any face to face selling; these are:

- **Stage 1** – Conduct a Benefit Analysis on the service or the product.

- **Stage 2** – List the Lead Questions to ask a prospect to establish to what extent benefits might deliver value, if any (Situation Analysis questions).

- **Stage 3** – Create a 'Strong Benefit Statement' consisting of words or phrases aimed at creating interest with the prospective customer, designed specifically to motivate the prospect to answer the Lead Questions prepared in Stage 2 above.

When the Payback Consultative Seller possesses the requirements as in 1, 2 and 3 above, the 'S' aspect of the ESPIRE® model can begin (Situation Analysis) once a prospective customer has been identified. In this example, a prospective customer would be every guest enquiring about green fees.

We will assume, for the purposes of this example that the Seller (the Pro) would know about all the alternative golf facilities in the area in terms of:

1. The logistics of locating and getting onto a course
2. The typical costs and options
3. The challenges and problems that are encountered by casual players trying to get a game

Benefit Analysis of Golf Membership

The Benefit Analysis would need to be completed using the Features as mentioned by the Pro in his demonstration type sales pitch illustrated earlier. The Benefit Analysis for the scenario would take the following form:

Features

1. Open access to the course seven days a week
2. Tee time booking facility available
3. Facility to enter competitions and events
4. Ability to obtain an official handicap
5. Full access to the clubhouse facilities
6. Cost £1000

Advantages of Features

Feature 1   Open access to the course seven days a week

Advantage   *Facilitates weekend play in addition to weekday*

Feature 2   Tee time booking facility available

Advantage 1   *Guaranteed tee time*

Advantage 2   *Avoids necessity of reporting to Pro Shop and the possibility that the course is full*

Feature 3   Facility to enter competitions and events

Advantage 1   *Provides ready partners to play with*

Advantage 2   *Facilitates play with better golfers to enhance learning of skills, rules, etc.*

Feature 4   Ability to obtain an official handicap

Advantage 1   *Facilitates play in official competitions*

Advantage 2	*Makes playing on other courses much easier*
Feature 5	Full access to the clubhouse facilities
Advantage	*Provides access for players and their guests to a range of social events and facilities to be enjoyed, sometimes at special prices*
Feature 6	Cost £1000
Advantage	*Unknown without knowledge of prospective customer's life and circumstances and the costs associated with playing currently*

Having conducted the Features and Advantages exercise, it is now necessary to complete the analysis of Benefits from the Advantages as follows:

Benefits of Advantages

Feature 1	Open access to the course seven days a week
Advantage	*Enables weekend play in addition to weekday*
Benefit	**Better options for time allocation to play, i.e. enhanced convenience**
Feature 2	Tee time booking facility available
Advantage 1	*Guaranteed tee time*

Benefit	***Time saving and eliminates the chance of 'on the day' disappointment***
Advantage 2	*Avoids necessity to report to Pro Shop*
Benefit	***Reduces hassle – saves time - convenience***
Feature 3	Facility to enter competitions and events
Advantage 1	*Provides ready partners to play with*
Benefit	***Saves time, money and hassle associated with organising partners to play with***
Advantage 2	*Facilitates play with better golfers to enhance learning of skills, rules, etc.*
Benefit	***Saves time and money in learning solely from a professional***
Feature 4	Ability to obtain an official handicap
Advantage 1	*Facilitates play in official competitions*
Benefit	***Ability to win prizes (Pro Shop Vouchers)***
Advantage 2	*Makes playing on other courses much easier*
Benefit	***Enhances pleasure and satisfaction from the game of golf***
Feature 5	Full access to the clubhouse facilities

Advantage	*Provides access for players and their guests to a range of social events and facilities to be enjoyed, sometimes at special prices*
Benefit	**Enhanced pleasure – image – convenience**
Feature 6	Cost £1000
Advantage	*Unknown without knowledge of prospective customer's life and circumstances and current costs of playing*
Benefit	**Also unknown as the Advantages are unknown**

Note: *It can be seen from this part of the analysis that price has no Advantages or Benefits that can be identified by the Seller without knowing anything about the prospect's circumstances. It can also be understood that quoting a price without knowing how a prospect would benefit is effectively asking the customer to work out the Advantages and Benefits for themselves with a high risk of a negative response.*

Having completed the first exercise, it is now necessary to evolve the questions to ask of a prospective new member to ascertain the potential Values of the Advantages and Benefits. Remember that Sellers need to create desire in the Buyer and it is only Benefits and Values that build desire. Readers might like to conduct an exercise themselves to evolve the questions to ask during Situation Analysis using the golf membership Benefits Analysis provided earlier. We have evolved and listed the typical questions to ask to understand the potential Value of the identified Benefits and these are listed below.

Readers should be able to follow how the Benefit Analysis was completed. In the event of any difficulties in understanding how it was constructed, refer to Part One. Once the Pro has evolved the Lead Questions, the next step is to complete Stage 3 by creating a Strong Benefit Statement. Creating a Strong Benefit Statement is picked up again after readers have digested and understood how to evolve and produce Lead Questions from the Benefit Analysis. We have also produced a list of questions that could be used.

Situation Analysis Lead Questions Evolved From Golf Membership Benefit Analysis

Feature 1	Open access to the course seven days a week
Lead Questions	*How often do you play golf?*
	Would weekend golf be more convenient for you?
	(Asked to ascertain potential value of weekend play)
Feature 2	Tee booking facility available
Lead Question	*To what extent does the paying of a green fee at the pro shop inconvenience you?*
Feature 3	Facility to enter competitions and events

Lead Question	*Would you like the opportunity to take part in competitions or events to enhance your involvement in the game and potentially win prizes?*
Feature 4	Ability to obtain an official handicap
Lead Question	*Does the idea of having an official handicap to enter competitions appeal to you?*
Feature 5	Full access to the clubhouse facilities
Lead Question	*Would you like to have access to the clubhouse facilities where you could take family, friends and guests?*
Feature 6	Cost £1000
Lead Questions	*How often do you currently pay a green fee?* *OR* *How much are you spending on green fees a year?* *Have you ever experienced not being able to play when you wanted to?*

As already mentioned, it is necessary to understand how customers currently operate in order to be able to propose a better way of doing what they do, if that is possible.

Having completed the Lead Questions exercise, the Pro would then review the whole Benefit Analysis exercise to evolve a Strong Benefit Statement in line with Stage 3 of the three pre-face to face selling exercises. For the purposes of this example, readers might like to think of and evolve a Strong Benefit Statement for the Golf Pro to use. We have created the following short statement for the scenario as follows.

> *"Part of my role as the club's professional is to ensure that all guest golfers have the best experience from the club in terms of pleasure and best value for money. Do you mind if I ask you a few questions which will enable me to ensure that you get maximum benefit from your visit?"*

The ESPIRE® model has now commenced with the Benefit Statement fulfilling the 'E' aspect of the ESPIRE® model (Establishing Rapport). Assuming that the guest provides a positive response to the Strong Benefit Statement, i.e. the guest has no objection to the Pro asking the questions, the Pro commences the Situation Analysis aspect of the model by asking the questions and listening to the answers to ascertain the extent to which a guest would save money and gain pleasure from accepting a proposal to pay an annual membership instead of paying the green fee. Once the Pro has received answers to all the questions, the Pro would have completed stages 'E', 'S', 'P' and 'I' of the ESPIRE® model, i.e. Establish Rapport, completed Situation Analysis, and identified any Problems (gaps) and the Impact of those problems, if any.

In this particular scenario, any problems that the guest might be experiencing that would clarify themselves during Situation Analysis might possibly take the following form:

1. The course might be busy when the guest turned up to play, which could cause a delay in commencing a game. This might be a problem if the guest has only allocated a certain amount of time to play due to the necessity to return home or engage in some other activity at a certain time. The impact of this would be dependent upon the circumstances of time constraints on the guest.

2. The guest finds difficulty in finding time to play during the week and, due to the unavailability of the course at weekends for guest players, the guest is not able to play as often as they would like. The impact of this would be that the guest can only play when the course is available and, therefore, possibly restricting the pleasure.

3. The guest has to organise a partner to play with each time, which may or may not be a problem, again dependent upon the circumstances of the guest.

Readers can see from these examples why the questions to ask during Situation Analysis are directly related to the Benefits of the product or service. In the three example problems highlighted, the impact of those problems, if they exist, would vary from guest to guest.

Let us also assume that the guest has previously played on the course three times a month for the last three months and is really beginning to enjoy the game. If this rate of play continues, the annual cost would be £1,080 (36 x 30).

The whole purpose of conducting Situation Analysis is to establish the circumstances of the prospect in terms of potential problems that might exist directly related to the way the product or service might solve those problems. Readers will remember from Part Seven that another way of looking at problems is to see them in the light of a 'gap' between what the prospect is experiencing currently and what the prospect could experience as the result of making use of the product or service. The impact of any problems or gaps identified by the Seller is the measure of the size of the problem or the gap. The bigger the impact, the more the Value of the Benefit.

Back to the golf scenario.

Once the Golf Pro has asked all the questions, a number of problems or gaps would be either established or not. If problems or gaps are identified, the Pro goes on to establish the extent of the impact. Having completed the Situation Analysis and established any problems and the extent of the impact of those problems, the E, S, P and I of ESPIRE® would have been completed.

Readers will recall from Part Eight that the R of ESPIRE® relates to Resolution Options. Let us assume for the purpose of this example that the Pro does establish that the guest does have time constraints and does find difficulty finding partners to play with, as identified earlier in potential problems for the guest. The Pro would further question the guest to establish to what extent these problems impact on the way the guest wants to develop their pursuit of the game. The Pro would establish that the guest has played three times a month for the last three months at a total cost of £270 (9 x 30) producing an annual cost of £1,080 (12 x 90). Readers will understand that the bigger the problems in terms of impact the easier it becomes to sell a solution by proposing the acceptance of the offering. In the case of this example, a guest accepting membership would resolve these problems, and save £80 per annum based on the guest's current costs.

The greatest payback proposition, in the case of this example, would arise as the guest could end up paying out more money on green fees than the cost of an annual fee. In these cases, no other arguments should be necessary to close a sale. It is important, however, to understand that ideally Sellers should ask all the questions relative to Situation Analysis in order to build the strongest possible case overall. It is very risky to jump to making a proposal based on one problem that is identified during the Situation Analysis phase of the selling process. That is not to say that a strong Payback Proposal cannot be made based on one problem if the impact of that one problem is big enough.

Golf Guest Situation Analysis

To finish the scenario, the Pro would complete the Situation Analysis by asking all the questions, establishing the problems and their impact on the guest. Based on the situation and the circumstances of the guest, the Pro would ascertain how to present the solution by offering the guest an annual membership. This is done within the Resolution Options aspect of the ESPIRE® model and is represented by the 'R' of the acronym.

In a commercial scenario, the Seller has an option of breaking off the sales process at this point (having completed the Situation Analysis) to return to their work place to consider the Resolution Options and to make any financial calculations and produce a written Payback Proposal. In these instances, the Seller should summarise the findings of the Situation Analysis to the prospect, highlighting wherever possible the problems (gaps) and the impact of those problems on the prospect's current method of operating.

In this example of the Golf Pro, the Payback Proposal would be made orally. In the event that the Pro was unable to identify any problems during the Situation Analysis (asking Lead Questions), the Pro would not make a proposal as there would be no basis for a sale. We have assumed that the Pro has identified some issues that could be improved as a result of the guest taking out full membership and would therefore make a Payback Proposal within the last 'E' of ESPIRE® (Economic Payback). As discussed in Part Nine, the Pro's oral Payback Proposal could take the following form:

Economic Payback Proposal - Golf Professional (orally)

"Based on our conversation Mr Guest it appears that you would benefit considerably from taking out full membership of our club. Here are the reasons ..."

The Pro, at this point, would explain how some specific Features of membership would improve the guest's current way of paying and playing and the key Features would be:

1. The saving of time by the guest having access to the course seven days a week without having to visit the 'Pro Shop', and the ability to book a specific tee time.

2. Weekend availability as a result of membership would provide the guest with much more flexibility. Also, being a member would provide access to potential partners to play with, thereby saving the guest the problems associated with finding partners to play with.

3. The key Benefit in this example is the cost as the guest would save £80 per annum and any additional games over and above three per month would be free. This saving is the Payback which results if the guest accepts the proposal to join and pay for full membership.

To close the sale, the Pro would merely ask the guest to consider this proposal and pass the guest an application form to complete. In the event that the guest will not or cannot make an instant positive decision to go ahead, then the Pro has the option of restating the Benefits at a later date as a follow up to closing the sale, emphasising each time the savings that could be made by paying a membership fee.

Part Nine shows how an Economic Payback Proposal in written format would be used in a commercial situation but Sellers can choose to make a Payback Proposal orally even in a commercial scenario, dependent upon the complexity of the customer's situation and the application of the offering.

We would recommend that Readers should review the preceding sections of this book several times in order to understand how to apply Payback Consultative Selling to any product or service, and acknowledge that considerable practice is required to overcome previous habits.

The following page summarises the key messages from Part Ten.

Part Eleven deals solely with the importance of understanding how psychology plays a major role in achieving success in the selling and marketing arena. Readers harnessing the power of controlled thought and all that this means, together with the Payback Consultative Selling Process detailed in this publication, should be able to significantly improve current sales levels and income.

Review of Part Ten

1. A state of 'Desire' must exist within the prospect to facilitate the closing of a sale.

2. Demonstrating Value and Payback reduces to an extent the customer's focus on the cost or price of the offering.

3. Sellers need to protect margins by using Payback Consultative Selling in order to fund their own costs plus generate a profit.

4. Closing sales is much more controllable using Payback Consultative Selling than by using the demonstration plus quote method.

5. The bigger the financial return over the shortest time, the easier it is to close.

6. Sometimes it becomes necessary to prove that an application will deliver the proposed results by the use of a reference site or a physical trial or demonstration.

7. Payback Consultative Sellers do not attempt to close a sale if they are unable to identify how an offering might show financial benefits.

8. Sellers have an option to return to their work place after conducting Situation Analysis in order to prepare a Payback Proposal

9. A sale may be closed by demonstrating how one Feature might resolve an identified problem but nevertheless full Situation Analysis should be conducted to ensure

that the strongest possible Business Case can be produced.

10. A Payback Proposal should include a summary of the whole customer situation together with how the application of the offering delivers financial benefits. This is done not just for the principal decision maker but for any third parties that might be involved in the decision making process.

PART ELEVEN - SUCCESS PSYCHOLOGY AND ITS APPLICATION IN SALES

There is now more information on the subject of success psychology than most people are aware of.

Scientists now know that every individual is engaged, knowingly or otherwise, in a self-fulfilling prophecy. Put another way, every person becomes what they think about. There are literally thousands of publications in the shape of books, CDs and articles written by scientists, professors, psychologists, scholars and gurus that prove, beyond doubt, that what and how we think delivers our future, both positive and negative.

Science focuses on the Natural Law of Cause and Effect to ascertain how anything and everything has already worked, or will work in the future. The extraordinary fact about this situation is that whilst the average person has in excess of 50,000 thoughts a day, a large proportion of them are random and negative. If we can accept that thoughts are causes, the simple conclusion is that controlling what we think and how we think must be of paramount importance if we are to create a deliberate future for ourselves.

This section is given over to explaining how thoughts are responsible for our destinies, and how to control our futures, which are hampered only by beliefs and habits. Beliefs and habits are simple words that describe in part how we have programmed ourselves unwittingly to operate on the planet, controlled from within by hard wired systems of which we are not aware. This section will not only make readers aware of how and why they see the world the way they do, but also to see that everyone has the capability to re-programme themselves for any level of success if they have the will, desire and methodology to do so.

So what are belief systems, why do they exist and what is wrong with having them?

Here is the news! Everyone develops a belief system. It is part of the way that humans are designed and we always have to have one although we may not be aware of it. Perhaps a good way to explain beliefs is to describe other phenomena called 'paradigms'.

Paradigm is a Greek word meaning 'frame of reference'. To survive on the planet, each human being automatically continues to programme themselves based on experiences. This programming designs the functionality of the filter systems in our brain, through which all events are passed, to establish a response. Animals develop this same instinct which enables them to decide whether to run, fight or relax given input via their senses. Clearly, the younger they are, the more the limitations on their ability to react accurately. Age builds experience and develops the filter systems to respond more accurately.

Humans are the same; they build filter systems over time. The problem is that different people at different ages in different environments build different filters and functionality and, therefore, different belief systems. Every event that occurs minute by minute causes the brain to filter each event to rationalise and produce an answer or a reaction. These answers cause us to believe the reasoning of the filters, which are known as paradigms.

If you follow the logic of these facts of how our brain works, you will also accept that what we see in the world is translated into the reality as seen by our filter which can only be equal to the extent of our experiences to date. New data, or experience, causes us to modify our belief system. We only need to look back over our lives to remember that the clothes, music and food that we liked some years ago we may no longer like. Part of this is fashion driven, but who drives the fashions? We do! Indeed, there may be things you like now that previously you did not like.

Before Galileo, everyone thought that the Sun revolved around the Earth and, indeed, that is what it appears to do. Galileo was ridiculed when he first discovered and shared with others that the Earth revolves around the Sun and that this fact, coupled with the Earth's axis being offset relative to the Sun, causes the seasons. Not long after these startling new facts were revealed, the world population completely reversed their beliefs to accept the real facts. This shift by masses is known as a paradigm shift.

We all stick with our beliefs until we change our minds due to new data or experience that we believe. This is very good news for companies and in particular, sales people. All prospects are people with a human mind that operates just like ours. They think, they feel and they deliver their lives. If they are managers, they think, they feel and they deliver their current results. Attempting to change a belief system or a paradigm is what sales people are paid to do. In short, change people's minds from 'maybe' or 'no' to 'yes'. Achieving this positive change requires a change of the customer's belief system. If a prospect thinks that you, or your product, or your price, or your company is something different from what is being sought, the answer is invariably 'No'. Do they know what they should be doing though to enhance results? Probably not! Payback Consultative Selling is the methodology for doing this.

People will often change their beliefs and paradigms if you know how to change the way they are currently seeing and thinking about something. If you show a prospect a product, or a service, and quote a price, you are allowing that prospect to make a judgement using their current data and beliefs. Hopefully, readers can see that whilst some prospects will come to the conclusion you hope for, many will not and cannot, given their current thought process. We have to convince them to see things differently, which is what Payback Consultative Selling is designed to do. The connection, therefore, with the psychology of how humans think, both sellers and buyers, is very real and very relevant - hence the title of this section of the book.

So what is the point of all this? Simply this: to progress towards having more control over our lives, both privately and commercially, we first need to understand that what we believe is probably not true in some instances. This would have to include many areas such as our views about people, relationships, organisations, work, behaviours, sales methodologies and indeed every aspect about which we have opinions, views, judgements and beliefs. So the first stage in developing a success mentality is to question our own beliefs about things, which immediately enables the mind to start to see everything differently.

Most people develop a limiting belief about their ability or right to acquire wealth and position which in itself is the main reason for the majority of the population leading lives of mediocrity or worse. Of course, there are exceptions to these generalisations, but we must have an open mind; otherwise we cannot break through the barriers of belief that might be holding us back.

In training programmes, we compare these facts about beliefs and paradigms to two examples, each of which will help you to rationalise with what is being said about beliefs.

EXAMPLE 1

If you put a live fly in a jar and put a top on it, the fly will try to escape by continually flying into the top. Eventually it realises that there is no way out and settles on the bottom of the jar. The lid can then be removed but the fly will remain at the bottom. The reason? The fly believes it cannot escape and remains contained.

Figure 21 – The fly believes it cannot escape as a result of failing to escape before

EXAMPLE 2

Young elephants in India are chained to pegs in the ground by one leg when they are small. Initially, they pull and tug to escape but to no avail. Later when the elephant becomes a full grown adult and is still restrained by the same thin chain and peg, it will not attempt to pull out the peg or break the chain because it has a belief or paradigm that it cannot escape.

Figure 22 – It's not the size of the man in the fight that counts but the size of the fight in the man; and that's all that counts

People are similar. They develop self evolved beliefs that totally limit their ability to succeed beyond their own vision of themselves. It is a fact that most self-made millionaires had no formal education and came from poor backgrounds which probably motivated them to push so hard that they broke through traditional barriers without noticing their existence. The fact is that we only need to raise our expectations just a little to rise above the average, and that alone enables us to progress faster than the average.

Let us focus now upon the other item that hampers progress, which is habit.

A habit is something we do automatically without thought as an automated function. This includes thoughts and actions.

181

Thoughts and actions are causes which result in outcomes. Again, it is simple logic to understand that if habits which developed over time are automated functions, they are in themselves causes and the same outcomes will always follow.

It is true to say that if we continue to do what we have always done, we will get what we have always got. If we want a different outcome, we have to do something differently. The starting point for change is thoughts and habits. We have to control what we think about and use deliberate habits to cause the outcomes that we desire. Those outcomes can be without limit. We can all achieve whatever we want depending upon our ability to think and develop winning habits.

Beliefs and habits exist in the subconscious mind. The mind is not the brain. The mind is made up of two separate entities, the conscious and the sub-conscious. It is important, in terms of controlling outcomes in our lives, to understand the differences between the two entities and how to use the differences to our advantage.

The brain is always switched on. It either works as directed or, in the absence of direction, will default to random. We said earlier that the average human has some 50,000 thoughts a day. Many of these initiate bodily movements but the rest are controlled to focus on something specific as directed by our conscious self. The brain works by association, which is why in conversation one person's comment leads another to follow on in a similar vein so each person in a group is motivating the continuance of casual conversation by this system of association.

Of the 50,000 thoughts, well over half are of the random type started by an association with either a previous random thought or an external event. It is also natural, for all sorts of rational reasons, for the mind to focus on negative aspects of our lives. In this context, by 'negative' we mean things that by our own judgement we do not like very much. So consider this – a large proportion of our thoughts are random by association and of the negative type. We already know that we become what we think about over time, meaning that 'thoughts' are 'causes'.

It is a scientific fact that your life to date is largely the result of past thinking. The good news is that once we understand and accept to what extent our thoughts are forming our reality, you can immediately start to do something about it, to start to design and build the life you desire.

The level to which you believe what has been said so far is directly linked to the way your mind has been programmed and the paradigms that exist. Some people for various reasons are so negative about their view on life that their quality of life is in a downward spiral as the result of the Cause and Effect that their thoughts and beliefs are delivering their future. On the other hand, many are so motivated by finding that the way to improve their life styles is directly connected to the way they can learn to think, that they go on to become senior executives in medium or large corporations or start up successfully on their own.

This whole publication deals with a methodology for selling in the future that can never be replicated by technology. You will believe and adopt the methodologies outlined to the extent of your belief and motivation to do better. So let us assume you want to move forward. How do we go about reprogramming ourselves?

The master key to success is Goal Setting. Most people in the selling business are familiar with goal setting but it has to be done in a particular way to harness the science of Quantum Physics or the Natural Law of Cause and Effect. More about Quantum Physics toward the end of this section!

Figure 23 - The Master Key to Success is Goal Setting

Before we deal with goals, together with the method for setting and achieving them, it will be helpful to understand how it is the subconscious part of the mind that works in mysterious ways to create our future. As you progress your awareness through further enlightenment of how the Universe works, you will be able to rationalise with this mysteriousness to comprehend how it really works.

Referring back to the 50,000 thoughts, scientists know that many of these thoughts are repeats of previous thoughts. The subconscious mind is programmed either deliberately or accidentally by repeat thoughts of the conscious mind. We can therefore understand that if repeat thoughts programme the subconscious mind, and if the subconscious mind delivers our future, it is easy to see how repeat negative random thoughts cannot be the recipe for success. The opposite of this is controlled, positive, repeated thoughts which focus on the future that we desire for ourselves.

As mentioned earlier, the only thing that hampers us from doing this, even if we become aware of the formula, is beliefs and habits. Here is a test. If, in twelve months time, your earnings, level of happiness, your self esteem or lifestyle are the same as they are now, or your future is controlled by outside events, you only have yourself to blame.

So let us concentrate on how we develop controlled positive repeat thoughts and to motivate ourselves in this direction. We can promise you that immediately you commence on this path you will be inspired and more in control of your life, which are the basic ingredients for happiness. You will create for yourself a sense of purpose and self reliance.

Let us start with "What is a goal?"

A goal is something specific and measurable so when you start listing them, bear this in mind. If they are not measurable, they become statements of intent and visualising them, which is part of the methodology, cannot work.

Many people argue that goals should be set against a time frame, but this is debatable in terms of personal goals because of the way Quantum Physics works. If you put a time frame on goals, you may time them too far away from the present because of the instinct to avoid failure. Business goals however should be timed, and on a very ambitious basis, thereby avoiding unnecessary delays. Goals should be prioritised in terms of what you desire first (short term), and they should be subdivided into long and short term. We would say long term is probably five years; medium term one year and short term is three months.

The next thing to know is that goals should be very ambitious and not connected to your opinions about how they might be achieved. All these things can seem illogical which is why the majority of people do not set goals and, therefore, achieve little beyond their beliefs.

Taking a quiet period to sit and contemplate what you would put on your 'wish list' if you had a magic wand is not only the way to go, it is also very enjoyable and will make you feel great even though nothing has at that point happened.

Having made your list, which by the way can be changed or added to at any time, the next step is to write down the reasons why you wish to achieve them. This is an important aspect of the mechanics of how you will go about manifesting your goals.

Next obtain pictures or hard copy images of the items on the list. If it is a car, for example, go and look at specifications, colours, interiors, options, the lot. This is an ongoing exercise and, again, this function is part of the mechanics of how it all works.

OK. So you have your list. Keep it private to avoid the possibility of people talking you out of anything. Once you have achieved your first goal as the result of this methodology, you can be more positive in sharing your enthusiasm, but remember we have to re-programme our beliefs, which will happen easily once we have proved to ourselves that we can manipulate our future.

Let us now get down to the methodologies of bringing your goal list into reality.

The first thing to understand is that pictures are the language of the subconscious. Intention, focus and repetition are the tools required to manifest your goals.

Figure 24 – Visualisation is the language of the subconscious mind

Every day review your Goal List and look at the pictures, imagining how you will feel when they are materialised. This frequent reviewing is the process required to programme the subconscious. Remember what was said earlier about controlling our thoughts? This is what is meant by frequent visualisation of our goals. Now, if you do not decide what to visualise, your mind will default to random thoughts which will also produce images and feelings and those random thoughts will materialise. Hence, the earlier reference to lives being either accidental or controlled.

So far, nothing has been suggested in terms of goal setting which is difficult, in fact, it is very simple, but the truth is that it is not easy. Why is that? The way we live, and particularly work, requires us to develop habits to structure and complete a typical day. These habits and structures take up all of our time. It is for this reason that changing our approach to life to facilitate the creation and achievement of goals is not easy. You need to make a very positive decision to start the process within the next 48 hours, otherwise too much time will elapse and your normal lifestyle will take over.

Ideally, initially you need to set time aside every day, at least fifteen minutes, to review your list and the pictures. This motivates you to then continue to think about them automatically in those 'dwell times' of the mind. When you review your list daily, you become motivated to think about your goals in a specific way during coffee and lunch breaks or whilst driving or, indeed, any time that you are not required to think about something specific as part of some particular activity.

The next two keys to manifesting your goals are activities concerned with visualisation and affirmations. Let us deal with these one at a time.

Every human being has the faculty of imagination and using imagination is a form of thinking. Many people have fears of one type or another, and with justification in many cases. Dwelling on these fears is a natural instinct but it is dangerous, as this dwelling coupled with emotion brings about the very circumstances they fear most.

Using our imagination to create pictures within our brain, then running constant pictures either deliberately or randomly, is what programmes the subconscious mind which does not use words as its language. Visualising is a deliberate and conscious decision to create a specific picture in the mind. Visualising ourselves with an achieved goal or an outcome starts the dynamics of manifestation. As previously mentioned, this is already working for you and everyone else. Our thoughts 'control the rudder and set the sails of direction' for our lives. To arrive at a pre-determined destination, we have simply to learn how to set the sails and control the rudder in a deliberate manner. It has been said that a person without a goal is like a ship without a rudder being driven aimlessly, affected only by the prevailing wind and tide.

The next key activity concerned with delivering our goals is known as 'Affirmations'. It is a little trickier to understand what these are and how they work but the rewards of harnessing their power are so great that it is worth the diligence required to perfect their use.

The word 'affirm' means 'to confirm'. An affirmation is a method of internalising through deliberate thought that a goal has already been achieved. The Universe and the subconscious are not concerned with time, which is a man made concept. You may have heard the expression 'the space/ time continuum'. This is a scientific explanation of space being infinite and time being eternal. Affirmations capitalise on this fact by programming the subconscious to accept that our goals are here now. Do not concern yourself with why this is so, as understanding how it works does not impact upon its effective use.

Here is how you use affirmations. Let us imagine that you weigh 80kg and that you set a goal to weigh 60kg. First you visualise yourself at 60kg frequently. Second, you stand in front of a mirror twice a day and use the affirmation that you already do by repeating to yourself "I am 60kg". This affirmation sets the subconscious into motion, the result of which is that you begin to see and react with your world in a different way, which causes the weight loss. In this example, you would probably fancy different foods and become involved in physical exercise, which are the causes of the weight loss outcome. The motivation, vision, plus whatever else it takes, occurs only because the subconscious has been programmed that way.

Two other points relating to goal achievement need to be covered and these are negative thoughts and failure. Failure is usually viewed as a negative outcome and is feared by most. The fear of failure is one of the principal reasons why people do not set goals. Failure, however, is good news! We need to look at failure in a different way; we need to see failure as being in an unexpected place, which is really what it is. However, you cannot be in an unexpected place unless you had an expected place to be. When we set ambitious goals we have no idea how our mysterious subconscious will navigate us there. Failure occurs because the causes we utilised did not produce the desired outcome. It is a fact that we can only achieve unusual outcomes by getting it wrong. Prior to the availability of global positioning navigation systems, navigation relied on trial and error. Whether in the air or on water, tide or wind or both will blow us off course. Navigators would calculate a compass heading, calculate some leeway by calculating current wind and tide, and set off measuring speed, distance covered and direction. By taking a fix with a sextant, they could fix their actual position over the ground and, based on the extent of their error, they would recalculate a course. Through this system of continual measurement and revision, they would eventually arrive at their destination (known as 'dead reckoning').

Plotting our way forward to achieve our goals works in a similar way. Every day, we should do something that will get us closer to our first goal, however small it may be. Look forward to failure as this means you are moving and, with modifications to your activity, the achievement of your goals is inevitable guided by our subconscious which has been programmed with the desired destination.

As part of the methodology for manifesting our goals, we have to avoid negativity. Negativity does a number of things which either slow down our ability to navigate to a specific destination or, at worst, navigate us to somewhere that we did not knowingly choose.

The man made world contains an inordinate proportion of negative conditions. We grow up in this world and the negativity affects our programming. This culminates in the natural tendency to focus on negativity, in short, things we do not like very much. Listen to conversations in public places, read the newspapers, negativity is prevalent everywhere and promotes and breeds further negativity, again due to the way our minds work by association. We need to protect ourselves from both external and internal negativity. It is a fact that thoughts lead to feelings, which can lead to actions and actions always lead to an outcome. Negative thoughts lead, therefore, to negative outcomes. When you catch yourself having a negative thought, stop yourself by replacing that thought with a picture of your favourite goal. We can only think of one thing at a time so use this fact to advantage.

Try not to expose yourself to negative environments or negative people. They both pull you down and act like an anchor on your progress towards your goals because of what negativity does to our subconscious.

As with Payback Consultative Selling, we train Success Psychology at three levels, providing our customers and delegates with the facility to progress through these levels. Each level is to be featured as part of the following publications:

1. The Quantum Leap to Payback Consultative Selling features Level One '**Success Psychology and Its Application in Sales'**

2. The Quantum Leap to Profitable Commercial Negotiating features Level Two '**The Importance of Harmony, Meditation and Affirmations**'

3. The Quantum Leap to Structured Sales Management features Level Three '**Quantum Physics – Harnessing the Science of the Universe**'

The section on the 'Power of Thought' is particularly relevant in the field of selling. We can learn all there is to know about the business of persuading others to our point of view but if we do not understand how to control our thoughts in the right way, we will be constantly struggling to obtain the right results.

Let us focus then on how the theme of this part of the book should be utilised to maximise your earnings and happiness from Payback Consultative Selling. We need to focus on a number of the elements of success psychology and these are:

- Attitude
- Goal Setting
- Habits and Beliefs
- The Natural Law of Cause and Effect
- Failure
- Time Management

Attitude

The first thing to do is to make a decision to adopt the teachings of this book for the purpose of improving your lifestyle, well-being and state of happiness beyond all recognition. You have to decide. Decision and commitment are in themselves a powerful cause. Decide also to review your current habits by looking at what you do on a daily basis in the pursuit of your work. Guard against the negative, both internal and external. When you decide to watch out for the negative, you will notice its many forms. This enables you to think about whatever it is in a positive way so that the effect that negativity previously had on you ceases. It is a fact that when you change the way you look at something, that something begins to change.

Start to programme yourself into seeing everything as an opportunity. Fight against any inclination to get 'fed up' with anything or anybody. It is important that you learn to keep your mind in a positive fighting fit state so that it can use its power for the right outcomes. Negative thoughts, bad temper, aggravation, arguments and criticism are all enemies of the successful mind. Initially, old habits to resort to these behaviours in certain circumstances are hard to break. When you wake up in the morning, look at your goal list, visualise how you will feel when you start to achieve them. Expect the day and meetings to go well. Decide to be 'nice' all day and smile all the time. It is a scientific fact you will feel good with these thoughts. Expectation is another cause and it works both ways. If you expect that a car park will be full with no spaces, guess what you will find. Expect to find a place and you will. If you do not, you're not supposed to be there for reasons which are usually elusive to our understanding. Developing a successful attitude is the first step.

From 'Think and Grow Rich' by Napoleon Hill (see Recommended Reading List):

> If you think you are beaten, you are.
> If you think you dare not, you don't.
> If you like to win, but you think you can't,
> It is almost certain you won't.
>
> If you think you'll lose, you're lost,
> For out of the world we find,
> Success begins with a fellow's will
> It's all in the state of mind.
>
> If you think you are outclassed, you are,
> You've got to think high to rise,

You've got to be sure of yourself before
You can ever win a prize.
Life's battles don't always go
To the stronger or faster man,
But sooner or later, the man who wins
Is the man who thinks he can!

Goal Setting

We are dealing with using success psychology in conjunction with Payback Consultative Selling here, so business goals are evolved in the same way as any other goals as dealt with earlier in this section. You spend a large proportion of your time at work so, ideally, you want that time to be as pleasant and rewarding as possible. Your earnings from your career represent the fuel to fund your lifestyle and to acquire some of the material things on your goal list. When commencing the identification of your business goals, you should first focus on how much money you want to earn in a year. Be ambitious with your first shot at this. It may not be overly ambitious to achieve an earning level of double your present rate after twelve months assuming non-capped commission. One thing is for certain, if you do not change the causes you presently adopt and do not set any goals for improvement, your earnings in twelve months will not change much.

Following the concept of setting long, medium and short term goals, you should start with your annual earnings goal five years from now and then set an earning goal for the next twelve months. The next stage is to set activity goals for existing customers and then new customers.

Take your existing customer list and think about what activities you need to complete to maintain or grow them. Calculate how much time this activity will take and allocate this time to your diary. This allocation of time to existing customers will enable you to plan some time to develop new customers.

The next goal relates to new business development. Think about how you intend to identify potential new customers with a similar profile to your existing customers. Think about the volumes and timings of revenues that will be required from new customers to support your earning requirements. When planning in this way, do not concern yourself with past performance or what you think is possible. Use the 'Aladdin's Magic Lamp' approach. You will have an opportunity to modify these plans as you commence your plan and discover that you were unable to 'crystal ball' gaze accurately. Remember that we will not be able to forecast circumstances accurately, in the same way as early navigation was unable to forecast wind and tide accurately. We have developed another simple acronym that is helpful to use when planning how to achieve goals and it is based on the word TIDE©. It works like this:

T   Think it (as described)
I   Ink it (write down your goals)
D   Do it (start the pre-planned activity)
E   Evaluate it (measure results against activity and modify causes and activity accordingly)

It is not possible to plan sales performance activities accurately in advance to achieve a particular outcome. The art is to start with a goal, then write down how you think it may be achieved. Hit that plan with maximum effort, knowing that you might end up in the wrong place in transit to your goal. You then modify your activity or 'causes' to close on the goal over time. When you adopt Payback Consultative Selling and the ESPIRE® model, you will be able to review the actions you took (causes) together with the outcomes (effects) and modify or change the causes by changing your approach to each aspect of the process.

Habits and Beliefs

A number of winning habits to nurture and adopt have already been mentioned. Be positive, smile, expect things to turn out well, be nice, give out first in order to get back.

Another worthy habit is perseverance. Be patient, do not expect the right results straight away; you have to learn how to perfect the right causes to achieve ambitious results. However, whilst being patient, do not give up. The world is full of people who are cruising with no goals. Your new approach will win out in the end.

The Natural Law of Cause and Effect

Perhaps you are beginning to get the idea how many of the things already covered in themselves are causes. The goal setting exercises enable you to establish the effects that you are trying to achieve. The mental attitudes, together with the processes and methodologies covered in this publication, are many of the causes. Go forward in the knowledge that when attempting to create a future for ourselves, we cannot possibly know precisely how to achieve it. It is merely a process of deciding what we wish to achieve, called goals or effects, and experimenting with the causes to perfect them. As thinking is the prime cause of everything, knowing how to think in order to harness the Laws of the Universe is paramount in achieving unlimited success.

Failure

Expect failure. It is good news. It shows you are moving forward but not quite on the right course. Henry Ford once said: "To succeed, it is necessary to double your failure rate". Develop the habits concerned with Payback Consultative Selling. Develop and perfect your skills in the areas of Benefit and Situation Analysis. Develop the habit of selling Value before Price. Develop the habit of using selling time wisely.

Regarding beliefs, this subject has been covered, but the biggest thing to remember is that your present beliefs are hard wired into your brain. Trying new things will deliver different results which creates a new experience which, in turn, modifies beliefs. Decide to go outside of your existing comfort zone and move deliberately into the unfamiliar methodologies associated with Payback Consultative Selling and expect to fail initially. It will not kill you and you will be surprised how pleased you will be with yourself knowing that you are on a journey of controlled wealth creation for which there is a small price to pay. You have to learn how to achieve it by learning how it does not work.

Thomas Edison carried out hundreds of experiments before discovering how an incandescent bulb worked. When asked how he persevered during all the failures, he replied: "I found out hundreds of ways that it did not work which led me to the right way".

However, in business it is necessary to build in damage limitation criteria so that failures do not cause a result from which recovery is difficult. For example, it is not wise to gamble the whole budget for a development idea without testing the effectiveness of the 'causes' (actions – activities). Another way of explaining this is 'wise gamblers would not put all their money on one bet'. - All In'!!

Time Management

This is an immense subject in itself and the principal lesson is that to succeed we must manage time and not let time, or the lack of it, manage us. Again, it all starts and ends with planning. Creating action lists without any time controls will certainly mean that time runs out before the list runs out. In the selling business, the principal challenge is centred around the short amount of relative time that we can be face to face with customers, or prospects, to influence them to buy from us. We have already mentioned the importance of allocating selling time between existing and new customers. Another prime focus for daily and weekly time allocation are the following key activities:

- **Goal Setting and Goal Reviewing**
  It is critical that you review your goals and the pictures of them every day.

- **Activity Tracking and Review**
  In view of the fact that failure is an integral part
  of success, it is also critical to track the results of

activity to achieve any required outcome to ensure that the right causes are being applied. If required outcomes are not achieved, the causes must be changed.

This section will have given you an insight into the importance of harnessing the power of thought for the purpose of improving earnings and lifestyle. This publication as a whole deals with the sales process that has to be adopted to improve margins and revenues in globally competitive markets.

Payback Consultative Selling and Success Psychology put together effectively represent the key for selling successfully in the future. Technology, no matter how advanced, cannot replicate the methodology of thought and process control as outlined in this publication to deliver desired outcomes, either in business or in private life.

Figure 25 shows the key mental components requiring permanent focus in order to guarantee success. We recommend that you write your key goals on a card and the key components of success on another and stick them in a prominent position to remind you to focus on them at the beginning of each day. Eventually, they will become imprinted on your mind and become a habit. Happiness, wealth, and a permanent feeling of well being will inevitably follow.

Good luck!!

Note: *the word luck can be used as an acronym meaning labouring under correct knowledge. We trust that the contents of this book have provided you with a enough new knowledge to avoid the necessity for luck in the traditional sense.*

Figure 25 – The Stairway to Success

Review of Part Eleven

Review Questions

1. Approximately how many thoughts does the average human have in a day?

2. What is the meaning of the word 'paradigm'?

3. What two aspects of human behaviour hamper our ability to re-programme the way we think?

4. What type of belief tends to hold most people back from wealth and ambition?

5. If thoughts lead to results, outcomes and effects, what is another way of describing thoughts?

6. How do we describe the nature of negative thoughts?

7. What is the master key to success?

8. What part of our mind delivers our future?

9. What function programmes the subconscious?

10. How do goals have to be specified?

11. What is the language of the subconscious mind?

12. How often should we review our written goal list?

13. What are two of the most important key activities to manifest our goals?

14. What is a positive way of describing failure?

15. When commencing the activity of setting business goals, what is the first thing to focus on?

16. How does one go about planning the development of new business?

17. What activities are associated with the acronym TIDE©?

18. Name three winning habits to adopt initially to commence a new approach to selling.

19. What did Henry Ford suggest was a method of enhancing our level of success?

20. What is the key Law of Nature that this publication focuses on both from a practical and mental standpoint?

Review Answers

1. 50,000.

2. A frame of reference.

3. Habits and beliefs or paradigms.

4. Limiting beliefs.

5. Causes.

6. Focusing on things or situations that, by our own judgement, we do not like.

7. Goal setting.

8. The subconscious mind.

9. Repeat thoughts of the conscious mind.

10. Specific and measurable.

11. Pictures and images.

12. Daily.

13. Visualisation and affirmations.

14. Being in an unexpected place.

15. Desired earnings for the first twelve months.

16. By reviewing the activity required to maintain existing customers and allocating a specific proportion of selling time to this activity in order to allocate a proportion of planned time to the development of new customers.

17. T= Think it; I = Ink it; D= Do it; E = Evaluate results.

18. Having a positive attitude, smiling, having high expectations, persevering, being patient.

19. Doubling our failure rate.

20. The Natural Law of Cause and Effect.

APPENDICES

GLOSSARY

ACCESSING – the process of gaining exposure or availability

ACCIDENT – an occurrence which was not deliberately caused; an accidental occurrence has an opposite meaning to a controlled occurrence

ALADDIN'S LAMP – a magic lamp featured in a children's fairy tale which when rubbed produced a genie who granted three wishes

ALL IN – a term used in Poker (Texas Holdem) when a player puts all their chips or money in the pot

ANALYSIS – the process of determining information by examination of the parts

BALL PARK – a modern expression meaning approximate

BELIEF – something the mind believes to be true or real and that it accepts with faith

BENEFIT – the positive deliverable or what the receiver gains or gets out of something

CAUSE – that which produces an effect

COGNITION - the process of perceiving or conceiving by the mind

COMPETITOR – a third party whose activity is directly opposed

CONDUCIVE – favourable (as in 'favourable circumstances')

CONTROL – the power and ability to cause a desired effect or outcome

CONVINCE – the ability to totally persuade

CRYSTAL BALL – a mythical ball made of crystal glass used by fortune tellers to see into the future

DELIBERATE – intentional; a fully considered action with intent

EFFECT – the result of a cause; an outcome

EFFECTIVE – an action or behaviour that causes the desired outcome in the most efficient way

EFFICIENT – to achieve an outcome in the most effective manner using the least energy, time or cost

FAB ANALYSIS – a process model which examines in detail the Features, Advantages and Benefits

FACILITATE – to enable or help something to occur

HABIT – a tendency or practice which is almost automatic and hard to give up

HARNESS – gear or equipment designed and used to couple up to something to gain access to its energy or output

INDUCEMENT – the process of attempting to bring about an outcome by leverage, persuasion or incentive

INEFFICIENCY – the inefficient use of resource to achieve an outcome

LICENCE – a verbal or documented authority or permission to conduct a specific activity which might be disallowed without such authority

LOW HANGING FRUIT – an expression used by Sellers meaning business which is the easiest to obtain, in a similar manner as it is easier to pick fruit that is low hanging rather than that which is at the top of the tree, higher up

MAGIC WAND – a cylindrical object, similar to a stick, used by magicians which, when waved, produces magical outcomes

ME TOO – a modern expression used to describe products or services which are very similar in specification to others being offered by competitors

NEGATE – to deny existence or to do away with the necessity

NO BRAINER – a modern English expression used to mean common sense or the obvious

PERSEVERANCE – to continue despite adversity

PERSUADE – to cause a change of mind or belief by convincing through argument or force

PROCESS – a series of stages or actions to progress to a specific goal or outcome

PROPHECY – a prediction of an outcome or an event at some point in the future

PROPOSITION – a formal statement putting forward a suggestion for acceptance

RABBITS OUT OF HATS – an expression used to describe actions magicians who present audiences with animals from hats believed to be empty, i.e. a magical act

RANDOM – without aim or purpose; something done without conscious choice, consideration or care of the result

SCENARIO – an imagined scene or situation of a future event

SEGMENTATION – the process of breaking down markets or customers to identifiable or measurable components or constituent parts for review or examination

SHARPENING PENCILS – sharper pencils make finer lines on paper and, in the context of this publication, it means making the price sharper or finer, both of which mean lower

SOPHISTICATED – highly developed, cultured or refined

STRATEGY – a plan of action or policy to achieve a specific aim, usually against a time frame

SUBCONSCIOUS – the part of the mind that is not fully conscious but is able to influence action

SYNERGY – the pleasant, active energy between people who share common beliefs and/or goals

TACTICS – the methodologies that will be used to achieve the objectives of a strategy

VIABLE – feasible from an economic standpoint

VICE – an adjustable clamp fixed to a work bench to hold material in a firm position

RECOMMENDED READING

- ***"The New Strategic Selling"***
  - Stephen Heiman and Diane Sanchez – Miller Heiman Corporation
  - Joint venture selling based on the win win concept
  - ISBN 0–7494–2833–3
- ***"The Seven Habits of Highly Effective People"***
  - Dr Stephen Covey
  - The fundamental keys to success
  - ISBN 0–684-85839–8
- ***"Think and Grow Rich"***
  - Napoleon Hill
  - A study of the most successful people in the USA
  - ISBN 1-59330 -200-2
- ***"The Greatest Salesman in the World"***
  - OG Mandino
  - You can change your life with the priceless wisdom of ten ancient scrolls handed down for thousands of years
  - ISBN 0-553-27757-X

- **"Accounting and Finance for Non-Specialists"**
    - · Peter Atrill and Eddie McLaney
    - · The basic principles and underlying concepts of accounting and finance
    - · ISBN 0-273-70244-0
- **"The Prime Solution"**
    - · Jeff Thull
    - · Close the value gap, increase margins, and win the complex sale
    - · ISBN 0-7931-9522-5

OVERVIEW OF 'PROFITABLE COMMERCIAL NEGOTIATING' TRAINING MODULE

The World of Negotiating

In today's oversupplied markets, most buyers will tend to attempt to negotiate price even when they have decided to go ahead against a quoted price or leasing rate.

It is easy to understand why buyers are motivated to do this, particularly in the area of capital purchases, and here are a few reasons.

Buyers know that most sellers have some degree of licence to negotiate price within certain parameters and, in certain circumstances, buyers first seek to establish to what extent licence might exist before exploiting it. Buyers also know that sellers who have licence will tend to use it if threatened with the loss of potential business.

Today's global competition makes it more difficult to continue to increase sales volumes and margins on those sales that are under price pressure. This situation has led to the intensive price competition that exists and causes organisations to protect their profits by following a strategy of safety to guard against paying more than they have to. These precautions take various forms including the issuing of edicts to their purchasing people.

These edicts may contain the following:

- Budgets do not exist as a matter of right and all purchases have to be justified by way of a Business Case

- Tenders or quotations from several suppliers may be mandatory

- Suppliers may have to qualify as a preferred source before they are invited to quote or tender

Many buyers have incentive schemes that reward them for money saved off quotations and tenders. Buyers know that sellers have to sell to maintain their employment and to add commission to any basic pay.

Organisations are also aware that it is easier to save costs than generate revenues, as the former is easier to control. It appears, therefore, that the trading arena favours the buyer rather than the seller. Small wonder that 'price negotiation' are words that most buyers and sellers understand well, but this is an arena where negotiating for buyers appears much easier than it is for sellers. There is, however, good news.

All organisations have to spend money in one form or another in order to continue to trade. Some of this expenditure is by way of fixed costs, i.e. salaries, wages, heating, lighting, etc. These same organisations are driven by competitive pressures to continually seek ways of improving efficiency. It is in this area where they will invest in order to generate revenues or cut costs or both.

Today's sellers need to know how their products or services can be applied to an organisation's particular circumstances in order to generate a financial return by way of generating additional revenues or cost savings on the present cost to produce products or services. This know how is often referred to as 'selling value'. As detailed in this publication, an understanding of how products or services generate value is an integral part of pitching price, which, in itself, is an integral aspect of negotiating.

The Negotiating Training Module contains customised industry scenarios to show delegates how important it is to sell value as part of positioning price to facilitate an improved negotiating stance.

ESP has evolved and trained a global negotiating process for sellers which has been well tried and tested, providing it is used in the right circumstances. Its whole purpose is to provide sellers with a process for protecting themselves from giving away unnecessary discount in circumstances where the buyer has decided to go ahead at the price quoted.

The ESP negotiating process works just as effectively for rental or leasing as it does for the purchase of capital goods. Ideally, delegates should have attended an ESP Payback Consultative Selling programme or studied this publication prior to attending a Profitable Commercial Negotiating programme or reading the dedicated publication on this subject, as price positioning and value form an integral part of protection from price negotiation.

The Principal Purpose and Objectives of the Training Module

- To teach delegates how to protect margins and close sales when the buyer is negotiating, and at the same time maintain the customer's goodwill

- To show delegates that the more they know about the customer's circumstances the easier it is to negotiate

- To teach delegates how to recognise and respond to subtle and sometimes extensive negotiating gambits used by buyers

- To show delegates how to use the well tried and tested unique ESCAPE® model to hide any licence they may have

- To show delegates the ESCAPE® model in order to help them protect themselves from giving away unnecessary margin to buyers who have already decided to proceed at the quoted price but still 'try it on'

PERSONAL COMPETENCY ASSESSMENT

The ESP Sales Competency Self Assessment tool is provided within the templates on the next four pages.

Readers are encouraged to study their level of competency in each of the four sections and to assess any gaps, if any, between 'Highly Effective' and 'Development Needed'. Competency assessments to establish gaps in skill and knowledge between the ideal and actual are often conducted by sales management. The ESP Assessment Criteria were originally evolved for sales management use, hence some of the measurements may seem particularly tough. Consider how your sales management might judge you against each competency criteria when assessing yourself to add additional interest to the exercise.

Each of the competency areas within the Selling and Persuasion category are covered in detail in various sections throughout this publication, and references are made to the other three categories, all of which represent a separate training programme and future publications.

SELLING AND PERSUASION

NAME: DATE:

	COMPETENCY CRITERIA	HIGHLY EFFECTIVE - A	MARK	NEEDS DEVELOPMENT - B	MARK	NEEDS EXTENSIVE DEVELOPMENT - C	MARK
1	Your ability to match your company's benefits and values to customer situations	You sell all services/products by converting all the relevant features to benefits and financial values that relate directly to the business goals/buying criteria of the customer to achieve maximum margins on a sale.		You are an above average performer through your relationships and ability to match stated needs with quotes. Could improve performance through justifying pricing with benefits and values.		Tend to demonstrate products or services with a quote and hope the customer will be able to calculate benefits and values.	
2	Your ability to identify the ideal customer for your company's offering and value proposition, for the purpose of growth	You grow the customer base consistently and effectively whatever the circumstances as a direct reflection of an ability to identify the type of operating circumstances that could be improved by the application of your company's offerings in value terms.		Tend to favour farming as opposed to hunting. You believe all prospective customers will be focused on price and difficult to access. Lack the ability to identify which unique aspects of your offering could be used as leverage if sold as a value.		Most new customers arise as a result of an enquiry. Very few new customers are self generated.	
3	Your ability to access decision makers	You consistently maximise selling time with key budget holders to achieve sales targets.		Comfortable with decision makers when called to visit, but you struggle to identify and approach key decision makers from a cold position.		Tend to take a comfortable position with either known contacts or people that will chat with sales people. Fearful of executive engagement.	
4	Your understanding of the benefits of your company's offerings in financial terms	You are able to demonstrate potential benefits in financial terms (measured value add) to the right people to the extent that they recognise it and embrace a proposal by investing in it.		Good understanding of the differences between features and advantages, but lack the polish of translating advantages into benefits which could be potentially measured for the purpose of financial value (ROI).		Insufficient knowledge of how products or services could positively impact a customer's P&L and therefore you struggle to sell financial value.	
5	Your understanding of how a business works from a financial point of view	You have a good working knowledge of P&L and Commercial Finance and how these are affected by sales gross margins and costs.		Possess a working knowledge of accounting but this is not translated into the presentation of a proposal or quote.		You have no working knowledge of commercial finance.	

NAME: _____ DATE: _____

NEGOTIATING

	COMPETENCY CRITERIA	HIGHLY EFFECTIVE - A	MARK	NEED DEVELOPMENT - B	MARK	NEED EXTENSIVE DEVELOPMENT - C	MARK
1	How often do you discount price without closing orders?	Rarely.		Frequently when under pressure.		Always	
2	What is your persuasion ability to change a 'No' to a 'Yes' without cutting price?	You possess a high level of negotiating skill and are able to identify customers who have decided to go ahead against a proposal / quote but who use negotiating tactics to gain further reductions. Therefore you frequently change 'No' to 'Yes' without excessive discounting.		Average ability through experience but you could benefit from specific negotiating training thereby avoiding unnecessary discounting to customers who have decided to go ahead at a quoted price but who utilise negotiating ploys to gain further reductions.		Limited	
3	How well do you recognise bluffing tactics used by buyers to force a reduction in price?	You are highly experienced and effective and you have had considerable training in this area		You are experienced at trading in highly competitive environments and you expect buyers to use aggressive negotiating tactics. However, you are unable to counter effectively with equal capability and confidence.		You have no practical negotiating experience and therefore you are vulnerable to discounting when under threat of loss of orders.	
4	How well do you sell value to maintain or increase margin?	You are very experienced and effective in translating the benefits of your company's offering into financial values and consistently achieve revenue and margin objectives.		You sell the benefits of the relationship and your company offering well but you struggle to translate these into measurable financial value and therefore often discount to write business.		You are unable to position measurable value before price and therefore you rely on standard demonstration with quotation and subsequent negotiation to close.	
5	To what extent are additional services / business terms or extras given away to close sales?	Rarely unless something is exchanged in return for a concession thus resulting in a win-win outcome		You will resist and argue against giving concessions but you will also capitulate if the loss of an order is deemed likely.		You are unable to resist or negotiate an alternative position and you capitulate within personal authority most often.	

TIME MANAGEMENT AND PLANNING

NAME:

DATE:

	COMPETENCY CRITERIA	HIGHLY EFFECTIVE - A	MARK	NEED DEVELOPMENT - B	MARK	NEED EXTENSIVE DEVELOPMENT - C	MARK
1	What percentage of available selling time is spent face to face or on the telephone with customers?	You accept the responsibility that sales resources are paid to sell and that their costs need to be recovered plus a profit to make them an asset. With this attitude plus diligent planning and time management, you maximise your selling time.		Whilst dedicated and committed to achieving sales targets, your selling time is often diminished due to a lack of planning in the areas of strategy, tactics, journeys, administration and communication. You do not readily appreciate the cost of time.		You are easily distracted by diversionary activity and therefore lose significant selling time, thereby not appreciating that time, once spent, is gone forever.	
2	To what extent is your sales funnel effectively sustained?	You diligently plan the effective management of the sales funnel by continually prospecting, developing new and existing business. You change strategy and tactics readily to achieve sales results by effective use of the sales funnel.		You understand the concept of the sales funnel, but due to inadequate time management and planning, you do not manage the sales funnel effectively thereby restricting performance.		You do not understand the sales funnel concept and therefore you are unable to benefit from using one.	
3	Do you operate with a documented sales plan focused on maintenance and development of business?	Regular segmentation of the customer base identifies current and future 'low hanging fruit', facilitating a measured and updated sales promotion plan which identifies activities for existing and new business.		You have a basic plan containing statements of intent, but objectives are not measurable and activities by time are not clearly documented, therefore any measurement of shortfalls with correcting activity is not possible.		You have no concept or understanding of planning and therefore operate mainly on a reactive basis and your performance is very much based on market demand.	
4	Is specific time with dates allocated to maintaining customers and obtaining new accounts?	You understand the importance of calculating the allocation of sales time to maintaining current business but leaving sufficient time to develop new business to achieve sales targets and you do this very effectively.		Some basic planning is conducted to ensure adequate maintenance of relationships with existing customers, but little time is planned or strategies evolved to develop new customers.		You have not had any formal training on the methodologies concerned with building a sales territory using sales funnel, customer segmentation, planning or time management. Therefore sales achievements are based on hard graft, market trends and luck!	
5	To what extent are Key Performance Indicators used and operated?	You have had considerable training and experience in the areas of ratio and gap analysis in order to evolve key performance indicators in the areas of tracking activities against time that will deliver the required results.		You rely on company KPI's to judge performance to date. You do not set personal KPI's to facilitate the changing of strategy and tactics to deal with any short falls in performance in order to achieve the company objectives.		Personal KPI's not understood or used.	

ATTITUDE AND COMMUNICATION   NAME: DATE:

	COMPETENCY CRITERIA	HIGHLY EFFECTIVE - A	MARK	NEED DEVELOPMENT - B	MARK	NEED EXTENSIVE DEVELOPMENT - C
1	Your ability to build rapport quickly and effectively with a new contact.	You possess a knowledge of how to communicate with kinaesthetic, visual and auditory personality types as well as understanding the technical aspects of deliberate body language and behaviour, in order to build rapport quickly and effectively.		You possess a sculpted personality enabling effective relationship building over time but could benefit from structured training in the psychology of effective communication.		You are learning the hard way through experience but possess no structured methodology to build rapport quickly and effectively.
2	Your ability to adapt and adjust your communication style to fit influencers and decision makers.	You possess the necessary knowledge to recognise the various types of personality and to modify communication to maximise desired outcomes, through training on personality profiles.		You get on well with like minded people but struggle with people perceived to be at a different level either financially, academically or culturally.		You operate automatically with no particular structured approach with little or no relevance to an analysis of personality profile.
3	To what extent are you self driven and motivated?	You are self motivated and maintain a high degree of positive attitude in a majority of circumstances and are able to keep cool and structured in negative circumstances		You require external motivation and ongoing sales management and coaching to maintain a positive outlook to achieve acceptable performance levels.		You look at the job as a means to an end with limited commitment. You rely on others for motivation and have a natural tendency to be negative.
4	To what extent do you positively view your company, products, pricing and colleagues?	You are extremely positive with every aspect of your company; you see the glass as half full and as the result of your great attitude you are highly regarded by colleagues.		You understand the need to be positive but sometimes struggle to reflect this attitude in your day to day activities. You would benefit from some structured training on the Psychology of Success.		You operate in a tough 'me too' market leading you to be negative about most aspects of your company, its offerings and the market place.
5	Your ability to set personal and business goals and achieve them.	You understand that Goal Setting is the Master Key to success and consistently demonstrate the power of this approach both personally and commercially by your ongoing use of the methodology.		You understand that the corporate world revolves around top level objectives but do not translate these into personal planning and goal setting with measured and timed activities. Your performance could be improved by utilising written goals, activities and measures.		You do not use the Natural Law of Cause and Effect and are therefore unable to set goals. The consequence of this is consistent shortfalls on the expectations of yourself and others which is demotivating and stressful.

Printed in the United Kingdom
by Lightning Source UK Ltd.
131579UK00001B/16/P